# Rising Above

## One Page At A Time

Inspirational Stories From Sheffield Hallam University Students

Published in 2024 by Discover Your Bounce Publishing

www.discoveryourbouncepublishing.com

Copyright © Discover Your Bounce Publishing

All rights reserved.

Printed in the United States of America & the UK. No part of this book may be used, replicated or reproduced, stored in a retrieval system, or transmitted in any form or by any means, electronic, mechanical, photocopying, recording, or otherwise, without the written permission of the author(s). Quotations of no more than 25 words are permitted, but only if used solely for the purposes of critical articles or reviews.

ISBN 978-1-914428-25-8

Although the author and publisher have made every effort to ensure that the information in this book is correct at the time of going to print, the author and publisher do not assume and therefore disclaim liability to any party. The author and the publisher will not be held responsible for any loss or damage save for that caused by their negligence.

Although the author and the publisher have made every reasonable attempt to achieve accuracy in the content of this book, they assume no responsibility for errors or omissions.

Page design and typesetting by Discover Your Bounce Publishing

# CONTENTS

| | |
|---|---|
| Foreword | 1 |
| About the University | 3 |
| A note from our partners… | 4 |
| Dedication | 6 |
| Bilaal Ali – Vision of my life | 7 |
| Charlie Fish – New beginnings | 12 |
| Chenhao (Mirror) Song – Boxing through barriers | 19 |
| Daniela Jevina – Becoming me | 24 |
| Dawn Thomson – A step towards changing your future | 29 |
| Doaa Ibrahim Mohamed – Glass child | 34 |
| Dominika Czaplicka – Overcoming limitations | 38 |
| Faith Ogala – The untold story of mentorship | 43 |
| Fatimah Adesanya – Be mindful of your inner strength | 51 |
| Gladys Awolowo – Beyond boundaries: navigating challenges, defying norms and inspiring success | 57 |
| James V. R. Oldershaw – Take the risk | 63 |
| Khaya Winfield – Breaking cycles | 68 |
| Mariam Oluwatoyin Adeboye – Persevering to achieve | 74 |
| Millennium Iyobuchiebomie – A familiar series of events, a wealth of specific lessons! | 79 |
| Oghenetega (Cynthia) Awharitoma – A journey of resilience and triumph | 84 |
| Olivia Ologbenla – No expiry date on grief | 89 |

| | |
|---|---|
| Oyenike Akinlabi – Realisation of a lost dream | 93 |
| Rashidat Kazeem – Life's crucible: shaping influences on my identity | 99 |
| Sopefoluwa Oluyide – Chasing the dream | 105 |
| Timilehin Moses – Aspect of life | 111 |
| Veengus Talpur – My journey towards my dream | 119 |
| Zainab Ata – My journey of 3000 miles | 124 |
| About TG Consulting | 130 |
| University resources and information | 132 |
| Helpful organisations | 134 |

# FOREWORD

I'm delighted to provide you with the opening for Rising Above; One Page At A Time and honoured to be the 'project Champion'. Throughout my career, I've had the pleasure of working with so many inspirational people, from all walks of life and with backgrounds far more challenging than mine. Having been born and raised in Cheltenham – a relatively small town in Gloucestershire, and probably best known for its horse racing – I moved to Sheffield in 1998. Despite a generous upbringing, I was the first in my family to access Higher Education. Education can always stretch our thinking, even more so against a backdrop of adversity and well-known barriers. Rising Above provides a striking insight into the latter.

My commitment to Sheffield Hallam University has been unwavering. Partly because my own vision and goals have been aligned, and partly because Sheffield Hallam has a mission to Transform Lives. But it's not the University that transforms lives, it's the people that work within the organisation – both staff and students. It's leadership, passion and enthusiasm of these staff that provide opportunities to challenge narratives, provide access and scale barriers. Opportunities that are grasped by our student body which affect genuine change.

This book will take you through many of these stories, one page at a time. Stories that motivate. Stories that challenge. And stories that show, viscerally, how lives can change. Rising Above showcases so many inspirational stories, it's unfair to single any one of them out. Yet some have crossed my desk, for some I have had the pleasure to share celebrations and for some I have been able to see the impact of their work with the many industry partners that get involved too. The book is humbling and should be a source of comfort to those facing similar battles of their own. However, shining a light on the challenges explored in Rising Above is only part of the story. I think that for those of us who haven't faced such adversity, there is an opportunity to seize the moment. To learn from those who have pushed against barriers and to be better ourselves in removing as many hurdles as we can, and by providing the right level of support to ensure that we can all be the best versions of ourselves.

By reading the book, you are becoming part of the story and gain the chance to write the next chapter as we collaborate to transform experiences, offer new initiatives, and scaffold the development of so many young people embarking on their business careers.

As a seasoned academic leader, I've written my fair share of books, but it's this one that will leave an indelible mark on your next steps. I hope you enjoy it.

Professor Rob Wilson
Head of Department
Sheffield Business School

# ABOUT THE UNIVERSITY

Sheffield Hallam University is one of the UK's largest and most diverse universities with a community of around 37,000 students, 4,500 staff and 295,000 alumni around the globe.

Our mission is simple: we transform lives.

We are an award-winning university, recently receiving Gold in the Teaching Excellence Framework for outstanding support for student success and progression.

We provide people from all backgrounds with the opportunity to acquire the skills, knowledge and experience to succeed at whatever they choose to do.

As one of the UK's largest and most progressive universities, our teaching, research and partnerships are characterised by a focus on real world impact - addressing the health, economic and social challenges facing society today.

We are ambitious for our university, our students, our colleagues, our partners, our city and our region. Our vision is to be the world's leading applied university; showing what a university genuinely focused on transforming lives can achieve.

# A NOTE FROM OUR PARTNERS...

What a privilege it has been to work with so many inspirational individuals, and to support and witness the culmination of their hard work and dedication poured into every page of this publication.

As partners, TG Consulting are proud to be associated with such a remarkable project. We believe that Rising Above, one page at a time, will not only resonate and inspire a wide audience but also, contribute to each reader's personal journey. The genuine voices or our authors and their ability to share their own journeys with emotional strength, shines through in every chapter, making every recounted journey told a truly valuable addition to this publication.

Collaborating with Sheffield Hallam Business school on this project has been a seamless alignment of values, and we take pride in knowing that this book will make a significant impact on its readers empowering others to share their own untold stories with confidence.

As partners we look forward to a continued commitment to breaking down barriers, creating opportunities, building confidence and celebrating the remarkable achievements and strength of students.

To the Authors, congratulations on this remarkable accomplishment. Congratulations on harnessing the power of your authentic voices to become courageous storytellers. Openly sharing your personal experiences is a testament to your bravery. I am honoured to have worked with you and excited for YOUR journey ahead.

Maria Esposito
Head of Partnerships, TG Consulting Ltd

*MEsposito*

# DEDICATION

This book is dedicated to every individual who has faced challenges on their journey and have risen above adversity. We hope you will resonate with the experiences shared within this book and find inspiration to implement into your own journey.

Remember that you will **_Rise Above, One Page At A Time_**.

# VISION OF MY LIFE
## BY BILAAL ALI

I want to share my story with you so you can get a feel of a disabled student's university experience and to inspire other disabled students and even non-disabled students in a similar position to me at university. I want to be an inspiration and role model for the university as a whole and anyone considering coming to join the university at Sheffield Hallam. I also want to share with you as I'm not normally the type of person to speak my emotions, but I would love it if you could get a feel of me as a person and how I cope with my challenges and difficulties in life. If I was to give one piece of advice to any student, it would be to take every opportunity you get and say yes to everything, as you can see in my story the amount of doors that have opened for me by doing this.

My name is Bilaal Ali. I am a second-year accounting and finance student at Sheffield Hallam University. I am also visually impaired and have a syndrome called Laurence-Moon-Bardict which affects my eyesight, weight and my learning capabilities. Being visually impaired has long-running effects on my day-to-day life, but I always try my best to overcome and achieve greatness.

Accessibility is something that has many affects on my overall learning, with technology acting as the backbone of my educational endeavours. Google Docs and Google Sheets have been lifesavers for me, with their intuitive design and fantastic accessibility options, I am now able to access my work the same as a student with 20/20 vision can.

I have also found that understanding module content at university can prove difficult, however, I have found useful strategies to overcome this issue, like taking my time with processing information, breaking down the information into topics and making the most of available one-to-one sessions with seminar tutors.

Social skills aren't exactly my forte and making friends is something that I have struggled with since coming to university. Confidence and communication skills don't come naturally to me due to my disability, however, over the past three months, working with my note taker Mason, I have progressed exponentially. Our chats about football, movies and music have rubbed off on me, and I was able to attend a networking event and speak to many business professionals and leave a lasting impression.

I am an avid sportsman, taking part in blind football and tennis, as well as boxing (not a specific blind version, and being blind certainly doesn't help me avoid a punch). I also enjoy swimming and going to the gym. These activities are a great help with my social skills as they put me in situations with multiple strangers with similar interests as mine.

I also have a community of people in a similar situation as me at a service for blind people called Sheffield Royal Society for the Blind where I go to do extra-curricular activities and socialise with other people. I attend this session with my carers who I see multiple times a week, our days usually consist of us going to cafés and cinemas with a healthy dose of football banter.

Whilst university has posed many challenges to overcome, I have also managed to make the most of the kindness found for students in my position from fellow students and staff members, who always try their best to help me whenever it appears that I might need assistance, whether this be holding doors for me, or giving me one-to-one help at the end of lessons.

My teacher Martin Roberts, has been particularly helpful, always making sure to read out anything he writes on the board out loud to make sure I am aware of what he has said, keeping to a good pace and checking in on me to make sure that I am following the lesson. These traits are so useful to a student in my position as it means I am never at a disadvantage to my peers.

In addition, I have also received great help from my other lecturers, such as Georgina Thornley, from my DPAS module, who has helped me with creating my CV, by putting me in touch with the Thomas Pocklington Trust and getting me work experience at the Financial Times.

Nick Hill, my employability advisor, has helped me by putting me in touch with Working Win, a company that supports disabled people into the world of work, which has been incredibly successful for me as I am now in employment at Nicholson and Co Accounting. This gives me a chance to get work experience in my field and get paid work before I have graduated university, and I now have a secured place to do my placement year in September 2024.

I have also been greatly helped by Alex, my tutor for business economics, who actively adapted to working with a visually impaired person for the first time, and in the process showed how caring he was and tried his best to understand my difficulties and support me with learning material.

He also nominated me for the Inspirational Student Award, something given to one student a year for their great work in the face of adversity; due to his nomination I won the award. This was a real confidence boost and showed my hard work and dedication to the course, and it was fantastic to be noticed by my seminar tutors and other staff.

My journey to employment has been greatly helped by the university, with doors now swinging open due to the help from those around me, greatly improving my access to exciting opportunities. I was guided immensely by my DPAS lecturer Georgina Thornley, who assisted me into employment by pairing me with the Thomas Pocklington Trust and Blind in Business, both of whom led me to gaining work experience with the Financial Times, which has opened doors for me in my employment progression and resulted in a two-page spread in the print and digital editions of the publication.

I was also helped by my employability officer Nick Hill, who helped me by connecting me with the company Working Win, who help disabled people accessing the world of work by assisting their accessibility needs. My connection with Working Win ultimately led to me finding employment with Nicholson and Co Accounting, who have gone above or beyond to help me with any extra needs I have with accessing the company in a successful manner. My employment with them also means that I have confirmed work for my placement in my third year at university, and that I will be paid for my time working with them.

My work with Nicholson and Co is different to what I had originally envisaged for myself. I originally wanted to work as a financial advisor, however, my current job sees me working with bookkeeping, spreadsheets, managing company/client accounts, handling invoices and calculating VAT; I have also been involved in a board meeting with a charity company called MCDT. All this new responsibility has made me feel essential to the team and made me fall in love with my working life.

My university experience has been fantastic so far, I am extremely grateful for all the support I have received from everyone around me, helping me in every aspect of my life. The support I have received has been plentiful and varied, with a great support network of module leaders and seminar tutors combined with my note taker/sight guide/study skills mentor, who helps me greatly and makes my days enjoyable, all culminating in a greater chance for me to succeed to the highest level.

# NEW BEGINNINGS
## BY CHARLIE FISH

In 2019, a year that promised new beginnings, I stood at a crucial stage of my life. Just after leaving high school, my ambitions were sky high, aimed at joining the Royal Air Force (RAF) as an officer and enrolling in the prestigious Welbeck Defence Sixth Form College. My passion for AeroSystems engineering, a field where problem-solving skills and technical insight converged, was the driving force behind this dream.

My path towards this goal was not merely the chase of a dream but a carefully planned and executed journey of sweat and tears. AeroSystems engineering symbolised a harmonious blend of my interests and skills, presenting an opportunity to make meaningful contributions to the RAF, an institution embodying discipline and innovation. The officer interview scheme of the RAF presented a formidable challenge, pushing me beyond my comfort zone while testing far beyond my academic knowledge. Leadership, teamwork and strategic thinking were scrutinised, and, albeit feeling apprehensive of the outcome, I embraced these challenges wholeheartedly, each step taking me closer to my goal.

The wait for the result was excruciatingly painful, drawing upon my patience and optimism to remain calm. Finally, the wait was over, and I was congratulated on excelling in the RAF's selection process, where I ranked fifth in the UK. This was a testament to my capabilities and hard work where I believe it was more than just a recognition that I was capable of completing the interview selection process – it was a sign that my aspirations were within reach if I remained focused and confident.

With grades as low as Level 3 in my GCSE mock exams, I realised how frustrated I felt with myself for not putting my utmost effort into my revision, and therefore I knew that improving my mathematical skills required more than sheer effort; it needed a focused and strategic approach. Tutoring sessions became a crucial aspect of learning, not just about mathematical concepts but about discipline, resilience and understanding my learning style. Hours of dedicated practice and problem solving were invested in building my proficiency for my GCSE examinations.

When I entered the school hall on results day, my emotions were running high; excitement mixed with insecurities provided a fluttering sensation within my stomach. Despite my dedication, my results fell short of the expectations, a mere three marks away from my target. I felt a sudden anger with myself, as I knew my dream had just been stolen from me. This shortfall was a major blow to my morale, a stark realisation that sometimes effort and outcome are not directly proportional. It was a period marked by introspection as I grappled with the emotional and mental impact of this setback. However, this challenge did not diminish my aspirations, but rather reinforced them when I finally reflected upon the grades I had achieved and realised they exceeded my expectations. I learned that resilience is not just enduring obstacles but using them as catalysts for growth. My experience with mathematics, both challenging and intriguing, solidified my determination to pursue a path intertwined with this subject.

Emerging from this experience with renewed purpose, I was able to finally see this supposed failure as an opportunity for growth, driving me to explore new avenues and enabling me to rebuild my hope and optimism to set another goal. It underscored the importance of perseverance and maintaining a clear vision, even amidst setbacks. This chapter of my life was more than an academic hurdle; it was a defining moment that shaped my learning approach and goal setting. It instilled in me the conviction that with perseverance and dedication, challenges can become stepping stones to success.

Confronted with the need to recalibrate my path, I turned towards Runshaw College and simultaneously applied for an RAF apprenticeship as an AeroSystems engineer, determined to climb the ranks from within. At this juncture, financial trading, which had been a peripheral interest for three years, began to take a central role in my life, evolving from a hobby into a deep-seated passion. After securing a place on the RAF apprenticeship scheme, I left college excited and ready to embark on this new venture, only to be met with another twist as the onset of 2020 brought unforeseen global changes.

The onset of the COVID-19 pandemic in 2020 threw another wrench in my plans. With RAF intakes postponed due to the whole world being in lockdown, I found myself needing to make a life-changing decision to withdraw from my RAF career pathway. A feeling of relief engulfed me as I made the call to my careers officer to inform her of my decision, although I felt uneasy in the pit of my stomach. During this time, I had found solace and purpose in trading. It was no longer a pastime; it became a lifestyle, a discipline that demanded and honed my analytical skills.

In this period of recalibration and self-discovery, I ventured into the realm of online proprietary trading evaluation schemes. This phase was more than just an extension of my trading journey; it was vital in that I consolidated all the knowledge and skills I had cultivated over the years. The challenge was to pass these rigorous evaluations and secure funding, a task that demanded not just technical expertise but also a deep understanding of market dynamics.

The proprietary trading evaluations were instrumental in refining my approach to risk management, an approach I realised was fundamental in the trading industry. Navigating through these evaluations, I learned to balance the fine line between calculated risks and potential rewards, an essential skill for any successful trader. This experience was not only about proving my competence but also about internalising principles that would guide my trading decisions in the long term.

Meanwhile, my academic journey continued to be punctuated with challenges, especially in mathematics. Enrolling at Cardinal Newman College to study mathematics, business and chemistry, I grappled with the subject that once stood as a barrier to my RAF dream. But with unyielding determination and an ever-growing appreciation for numbers, I turned my weakest link into one of my greatest strengths. Dedicating additional time to my studies to access private tutoring led to the proud achievement of all my A-Levels at higher-than-expected grades, which provided me with the offer of a place at my first-choice university to study financial trading and investment management. trading, in these formative years, was more than a venture; it was an opportunity that has supported me to shape my resilience. The world of finance is unforgiving, often brutal, and always unpredictable. Yet, in this volatility, I found my rhythm, learning the art of patience, strategy and risk management. I aimed to take all that I had learned throughout my earlier journey and put it into practice throughout my degree.

Sheffield Hallam University marked the next phase of my journey, where I dove deeper into the realms of finance and economics. My days were a blend of academic rigor and trading, each reinforcing the other. Trading was not just a practical application of my studies; it was a real-world test of my perseverance and strategic acumen. Embarking on the Level 5 Advanced Diploma in Financial Trading marked a pivotal moment in my professional journey, one characterised by significant growth, learning and transformation.

One of the most significant challenges I have faced during my recent studies was adjusting to the shift in market volatility, moving from FX to Futures trading. This transition demanded not only technical adaptability but also an enhanced focus on emotional discipline and decision-making. I learned to maintain composure and adhere to a disciplined trading approach. This period of intense learning and application was instrumental in solidifying my understanding of professional trading platforms and the broader financial landscape.

As I look back over my journey so far, I see these experiences not as setbacks but as invaluable lessons. They have equipped me with a deeper understanding of the trading industry and a more mature approach to managing the psychological aspects of trading. This journey has been a transformative one, turning challenges into learning opportunities and shaping me into a more proficient and grounded trader.

These experiences, while challenging, have been immensely instructive. They have taught me the importance of a balanced mindset in trading, where emotional control and psychological resilience are as crucial as technical astuteness. The journey through proprietary trading evaluations was more than just a quest for funding; it was an enlightening path that shaped my understanding of trading as a serious and disciplined profession.

I recognise that my primary challenge was not in the mechanics of trading, but in the psychological aspects of it. The retail trading space, often misconceived as a quick route to wealth, had initially skewed my perspective, leading to several setbacks. The allure of quick gains was a tempting narrative, but it was also misleading, masking the true nature of trading – a field where patience, strategy and discipline are paramount.

Now, as I set my sights on the Certificate in Quantitative Finance (CQF), the Chartered Financial Analyst Accreditation (CFA) and a master's degree in finance, I look back at my journey with a sense of pride and accomplishment. The skills and experiences gained during the RAF selection process highlighted my key areas for development and made me aware of my strengths. My previous academic struggles and the immersive experience in trading have coalesced into a singular, aspirational vision: to excel in the world of finance as a professional trader.

My journey is a testament to the belief that with unrelenting effort and a passion for learning, every challenge can be transformed into an opportunity – don't allow a setback to stop you in your journey and use your barriers to overcome your failures and succeed in your strengths.

# BOXING THROUGH BARRIERS
## BY CHENHAO (MIRROR) SONG

We must face many choices in life; some choices lead to change, and change often means challenges, which sometimes make us suffer.

My journey has taught me that:
Pain + Reflection = Progress
Maybe you feel the same?

## My journey

My journey began in a small city in northeastern China; it took me from Beijing to Shanghai and to the vibrant city of Sheffield, England, where I completed my undergraduate degree (accounting and finance) with a high 2:1 qualification (68%) at Sheffield Business School. The quest for knowledge didn't stop there; I pursued my first master's degree (finance and management) at Adam Smith Business School in Glasgow, Scotland. With a thriving career in the headquarters of a six-billion-euro annual sales insurance company housed in the iconic Shanghai Tower (the third tallest building in the world), life seemed settled. However, at the age of 30, a burning desire for change led me to Finland, where I embarked on a new adventure and pursued a second master's degree in marketing.

The tapestry of my life has been woven with threads of change, adaptation and growth. Each city I've lived in forced me to encounter diverse people and situations, compelling me to step out of my comfort zone. This continuous cycle of new challenges, whether crowned with success or fraught with failure, has been my school of life, shaping not just my understanding of the world but also molding my character. Japanese fashion designer Yohji Yamamoto said that the "self" is invisible; bumping into something else, bouncing back, will allow you to understand the "self", so when you collide with something very strong, something terrible, something of a very high standard, then you know what "you" are and this is the "self".

## Critical changes

My life is full of changes, among which three experiences significantly impacted on me. The first change was when I ventured from a small city to the prosperous capital of Beijing when I was 14. The unintentional ridicule from my classmates and the unfamiliar environment troubled me. I couldn't sleep at night. I sat on the bed and looked at the sky through the window, feeling lonely and scared. The desire to persist allowed me to survive the initial stage, and for the first time, I felt the need to adapt in the face of change.

The second change occurred when I was 19; when I entered a college in Shanghai, I faced the cultural differences between northern and southern China. This made me understand for the first time the pain and confusion that comes when reality differs from your expectations. But as I began to understand other people's perspectives and accept new realities, this initial discomfort and pain transformed into an opportunity for growth.

The third change was when I started studying in the UK at 21. Although I learned English for many years and knew a little about the UK before coming here, the cultural shock and language barrier remained. In the first three months, I mainly chose to stay in my comfort zone, which meant going to uni and having fun with my compatriots. One day, I asked myself: is this the purpose of coming here, away from home? I woke up and pushed myself out of my comfort zone. Through sports and hobbies, I have explored unknown cultures, developed friendships, improved language and built mutual understanding.

## Challenges at SHU

While at Sheffield Hallam University, I have been presented with challenges that exemplify the spirit of resilience. For example, the decision to try boxing was an entirely new venture for me; I had never attempted boxing in the past 21 years before coming to the UK, nor had I seen a complete match on TV, but I knew that Britain was the home of boxing. When I saw the gym timetable at the university and there were boxing sessions, I thought: why not try it? The funny thing is that I went to the wrong session the first time. When I found out that I was the only male in the session, I felt something was wrong. Later, I realised it was a boxing fitness session, but I still finished the class happy and sweating. The second time I participated in the proper boxing session, I was the only Asian. I couldn't understand the warm-up instructions from the beginning because they were technical terms, but I could see and imitate them. Since then, I have participated in almost every class and have a mentality of representing China during training, so I can't give up. Sometimes, I am so tired that I can't open the door when I go home, but I have made many new friends, participated in the election a year later, and joined the SHU: BOX committee to help more people.

## Choosing Finland

At 18, the loss of my grandfather proved to be a poignant turning point. It illuminated the transient nature of familial companionship and instilled a profound understanding that life waits for no one. The regret of not spending enough time with him fueled a commitment to live a life without regrets. This philosophy led me to think carefully about the consequences of my choices, accepting both positive and negative outcomes as opportunities for learning rather than succumbing to regret. My biggest challenge at the moment is to give up my life, work, friends and family in Shanghai and come to a new environment in Finland to start a new chapter in my life and pursue my dreams and passions. It underscores the importance of embracing change, even when it requires leaving behind the familiar.

## Advice for you

To the students navigating the uncharted waters of a new environment as they embark on their university journey, juggling multiple roles – student, friend, family member and more – parallels my experience. The challenges may vary, from getting a high score to collaborating on group projects. As you stand on the precipice of the unknown, take the first step with confidence, knowing that every challenge is an opportunity, and every adaptation is a step towards a more enriched version of yourself.

My journey encapsulates a relentless pursuit of change, adaptation and growth, fostering traits of curiosity, flexibility and persistence. If these qualities resonate with you, let my experience inspire your initial steps, assuring you that the journey, once begun, holds no room for regrets. As Michael Jordan aptly stated, "Limits, like fears, are often just an illusion."

May your journey be transformative and fulfilling, your curiosity will fuel your exploration, courage will propel you forward, and perseverance will prevent you from giving up.

## Special thanks to Damion Taylor

Acknowledging the impact of my journey wouldn't be complete without expressing gratitude to Damion Taylor, my course lecturer and friend at Sheffield Hallam University. His mentorship transcends geographical distances, demonstrating the lasting impact of meaningful connections. It's a testament to the bonds formed and the enduring influence of those who guide and inspire. He is the one who introduced me to this opportunity to share my story, and he is the reason that I still connect with SHU after ten years.

# BECOMING ME
## BY DANIELA JEVINA

Why me? It's a question that has followed me all my life, through the highs and lows. I moved to England when I was only seven years old. I didn't know the language and didn't have any friends; all I had to look forward to here was my mum as I had grown up mostly with my grandma back in my home country. I remember it like it was yesterday... the tears, the pain of trying to settle in, trying to fit in. I was never the smartest kid, nor was I popular. I was just always trying my best, as my only dream was to make my mum proud of me.

My mum had sacrificed so much and worked so hard to make sure I could get a good education and a good life. She has always been an inspiration to me in many ways, from her dedication to work to always being loyal and authentic. Throughout my childhood, my mum worked very often, and I didn't see her a lot. However, she has really shaped me into the person I am today, from my work ethic to my personality and respect for others, for which I will be forever grateful.

Since I was young, I was determined I wanted to study law and criminology and become a barrister one day. I guessed this desire came from it being a respected profession that would pay a good income.

Therefore, I had chosen respective A-levels to aid me in getting into university to study this. However, little did I know what was creeping up on me.

## COVID-19...

COVID-19 has changed many lives; it's as if the world had almost stopped, and life has not been the same ever since. This has been the case for me; my life took a great turn and I never got to sit my A-levels, I lost my job because the branch closed down, and I spent endless days at home. Despite this, I was still determined to follow my plan and go to university to study law and criminology. Yet when I came here, I was deeply humbled and lonely. All my expectations came crumbling down as we had entered another lockdown and everything moved back online.

I didn't last long. After two months, I moved back home and went to work in a factory as a print room operative. Being in Sheffield, studying online full time, was a very lonely and depressing time for me as I didn't make any friends from my course; I didn't get to have the full fresher experience or enjoy the fun of living in a big town such as Sheffield.

As time went on, I continued working and attending online learning, but with every lesson, I was becoming less and less interested. Something I had been dreaming of from such a young age had become something I dreaded to study and even look at. During every online lecture, every online seminar, my only thought was of when can this end. I stopped engaging with the material and chose to start prioritising my work over university as that brought me joy; I genuinely loved going to work and became very passionate about it.

At the end of my first year of studying law and criminology, I had failed most of my exams and coursework and would need to resit the year if I wanted to continue. That's when I decided to take a gap year to refocus on myself because I had never had this sort of slacking approach to studying. That's when I was offered a great opportunity to progress in my work to become a production administrator, which changed my life so much. Despite it being hard at the beginning, I fell in love with this position and became very passionate about it. Slowly, the lockdown and the restrictions began to ease, and life began to feel like as it had before.

Thanks to this good job, I have met the most helpful and amazing co-workers, they have truly become like a family to me and allowed me to gain so many skills and build myself up. It opened my eyes to something I had always loved since I was young, but had neglected as something to pursue a career in – maths.

Returning to university was very hard; in the year off, I had gained a good job, a loving relationship, financial stability and friendships. Going back would mean leaving that behind and stepping into the unknown again, or worse, going through the same experience, which left me in not the best state as it made me question myself a lot, not only in my academic proficiency but also in my mental health.

## But I took that step…

I took the step, left everything back in my hometown, and moved back to Sheffield to study accounting and finance. At the very last moment, I decided to just go for it. And I could not thank myself enough for that step.

Starting all over again was daunting as all I could think back to was my past university experience and, at the same time, my life back at home and how stable and good everything was. A lot of people underestimate how truly lonely university is at times, regardless of how many friends you have. It is the first time of true independence, and it is terrifying.

However, I began to enjoy studying again on the accounting and finance course, and feel like myself again. Even though it is hard to study when English is not my first language, I still try my best, and I still do my job part time during the holidays. I am blessed to be supported by my boyfriend, my family and my friends in every way. I am very fortunate in life for the people around me. I work hard for everything in my life, but I'm not rich in money; I'm rich by being surrounded by pure love and support. My greatest blessing in life, of course, is my mum. She doesn't realise it, but she really is my rock.

At times, I do wonder what my life would look like if COVID-19 never happened. Would I be as happy as I am today? Would it be worse? Questions that will never get answers, and quite frankly, it doesn't matter.

If you don't face challenges and shortfalls, you will never grow. So, every trip along the way made me able to take a greater leap in the long run and be grateful for everything in my life. I have always believed that kindness and good deeds return as a boomerang, which I live by. Ultimately, I look at the past not with resentment but with passion, as I know that my past has made me who I am today.

We are often blind to how lucky we are in life as we tend to envy others for their success, family, lifestyle etc. So, I hope that by reading this, as well as other people's stories within this book, you can take the time to reflect on your own life and yourself. To see the good and the bad in your own life and be proud of yourself that you've made it this far. We all fight our own battles in life, we all make mistakes, at the end of the day we are all people that are just trying to find themselves. Once you can reflect on yourself, you can grow as a person and realise everything happens for a reason in life.

One thing I would want you to take away from my story is that life is too short. We underestimate how short life really is while we are young and therefore are ungrateful for the little things in life. Life is too short not to be happy, to hold grudges, to not take risks; life is simply too short to not be yourself. We only live once, make it memorable, stay humble and be grateful.

Lastly, one of my favourite artists has a very powerful quote that I wanted to share:

"Я живу я творю я смеюсь я мечтаю" – Miyagi

Translation: "I live I create I laugh I dream" – Miyagi

# A STEP TOWARDS CHANGING YOUR FUTURE
## BY DAWN THOMSON

I am a mature student (currently 27 years of age) and have previously spent six years working in early years childcare, since the COVID-19 pandemic I have had my own child (now three years of age), which pushed me towards taking the steps into a new career path. I had wanted to change careers for some time and began an application to Sheffield Hallam at the start of 2020, which I never submitted out of fear, hesitation and self-doubt. Am I smart enough to be accepted? What if I fail? Do I have enough money? But, with the arrival of a baby shortly ahead of me, I could have either stayed unhappy in my current stable childcare job or taken the risk to better myself and my family's future. That's why I finally committed to applying for Sheffield Hallam in 2021.

Ever since secondary school I had really enjoyed maths, but also enjoyed the idea of teaching. I felt I had very little guidance towards making the best decision for the future and so I opted for pursuing a Level 3 CACHE diploma in early years childcare rather than going down the A-Level route (again, I was doubting my academic capability). At the time I genuinely thought it was the right decision for me, and with no regrets, it taught me a lot about myself and has given me the necessary skills to build working relationships. But, as enjoyable as my job once was, it was no longer giving me a sense of fulfilment and I strived to develop more.

Fast forward to September 2021, I enrolled onto the accounting and finance course with a foundation year and optional sandwich placement. The sense of achievement I felt when I had been accepted onto this course was like no other. I had been brought up to believe that university was too expensive (it was for the posh kids) and something so out of reach that I needn't bother striving for it, that I should finish college and get a job, where I would then spend a decade or more working my way up the "ladder". That stigma that had been embedded in me since childhood was now broken, because I got accepted into university; I didn't need to be in a certain financial position, I was smart enough and the only reason I could ever fail is if I let myself, and that was not an option. The letter of acceptance, in my eyes, was all the encouragement I needed to believe in myself, regardless of the doubts that crossed other people's minds.

Starting university life was a breath of fresh air. I love putting my efforts into learning new things and enhancing my personal development, it gives me a sense of achievement and confidence, some self-worth that reassures me that I am good enough to achieve what I set out to do. I can't lie, at first it was daunting, I was around six years older than most of the other students, along with having a 10-month-old infant. I felt as though I'd stick out like a sore thumb and that I was alone in my journey in a sense that no one else around me could relate to, other than some of the tutors. I soon realised there are so many provisions in place that help smooth the bumps in the road. Having the childcare grant is one of the most helpful, as I have little to none immediate family that could look after my daughter while I studied. Having a safe place to drop her off where she could also continue to develop was one less thing to worry about, and having the help from the childcare grant to cover most of those costs was a life saver. It was something I never even thought about when I initially applied, but I don't know where I'd be without it. The flexibility of my university timetable also contributes to making my life easier, as I can request to alter the times of my seminars so I'm able to pick my daughter up from nursery. The support provided by the university and available grants have not only provided me with room to breathe, they have made me feel like I am more than capable of achieving the degree I am working so hard towards. It reassures me that I am meant to be here and that there are so many others embarking on this journey in similar circumstances to myself.

The restrictions of everyday life for me as a mum and full-time student have given me many challenges, one of them being that I am limited to when I can fit in independent study time. Although, enrolling for the foundation year enabled me to gain an insight as to how exactly I can work my home life around my studies and vice versa. After having a large break in my academic journey, the foundation year also eased me back into my academic studies. After having many sceptical thoughts of whether university was the right path to take, I felt so relieved with how well I was handling the big changes that were coming my way, not to mention the confidence and self-empowerment that had grown since enrolling.

Though motivational speeches, knowledge, advice and encouragement are things many parents feed into their children, it's something I never experienced much growing up. Instead, I grew up with self- doubt and lacking confidence. However, the support received by the tutors and the students you meet who are in similar positions to you, tell you that you do have the potential and that there are people that believe in you. If, like mine, your family are doubting the opportunities within university and the long-term benefits, but they themselves are not in the position that you want to be in at their age, then strive for what you want to achieve. Because your life is all about you and how you want to live, after all, that's all that really matters.

Reflecting on my journey, a piece of advice I'd give to my 16-year-old self would be to never limit yourself and settle for less. Don't let the decisions of your family and others determine how successful you will be in life. Instead, really think about what it is you want to do and what you want for your future. Don't be afraid to ask all the silly questions that you think will make you appear uneducated, because the answer to those questions could have a real impact on the decisions you make. I am constantly craving knowledge, the more I know, the more my confidence rises. I guess I tend to think this way because I was never a "cool kid", never followed all the trends the other kids did, e.g. the Blackberry phones, the popular branded shoes etc. I always felt so held back by my lack of popularity and family's financial position that I had little self-importance and so, as I mentioned previously, I settled for the easier option because I thought that's all I was capable of. Turns out I was wrong, through extreme dedication, I am soaring through my modules at university and enjoying the beauty of what I can achieve when I really put my mind to it.

I was inspired to share my story with you in hopes that it may give you a little light in the darkness, a little courage to be bold and brave. After all, you are your biggest critic in life and only you can limit your potential. Maybe you're reading this and wondering where you would have been if you decided to set goals towards following your dreams instead of merely dreaming them. Maybe you've been feeling stagnant for so long that making any changes in your life is scary because what if it doesn't work out? I'm here to tell you from experience that it is never too late to embark on new adventures and that it is far riskier remaining stagnant in life than it is taking a chance on yourself and making changes towards what you really desire. You may think you don't have any support around you to be able to make those changes, I know that's what I told myself for many years, until I realised I was the only support I needed to set the goals, and that if I truly wanted to achieve them, then I would. Of course, this changed once I started university and I am now surrounded by support, from tutors that truly care about my success, to careers advisors, academic advisors and more. University is a sea of opportunity, where you are surrounded by like-minded people all striving for successful futures. So don't let your past determine your future, because you have the potential to do so much more. And you can take those steps towards changing your future for the better.

# GLASS CHILD
## BY DOAA IBRAHIM

The chapters of my life unfolded like pages in a well-worn book, each revealing a new adventure, a lesson learned and a piece of the person I was destined to be. Hi, I'm Doaa and this is the story of my life. I grew up in a small town in the East Midlands called Derby. My parents migrated here in 2001 with my eldest sister, I wasn't here yet so unfortunately they were not graced by my presence. The reason for their migration was to seek medical treatment for my sister who had a kidney disorder. Later, she was eventually diagnosed with severe autism and learning difficulties. The discovery had put a strain on both my parents as they were also trying to navigate moving away from our home country, Sudan, as well as taking care of my sister. While growing up, I had to take on the role of a responsible older sister even though my sister was older than me.

Children are meant to be outside having fun and enjoying their childhood, unfortunately, this wasn't the case for me. I found myself having more responsibility on my shoulders. Whenever we went out for playdates and shopping with our parents, I would have to watch and make sure my sister was okay. This gave me a sense of protectiveness as

I had to constantly keep a watch on her. As we got older, her condition worsened as she developed a kidney disease. This caused our family stress as we were constantly moving around different hospitals trying to get her treatment. She was put on a waiting list to get a kidney transplant. In the meantime, she was put on dialysis in Thomas Cromwell Hospital in London. This caused us to move back and forth from London to stay together as a family while my sister was getting treatment.

When I was four years old, my mum and I went on holiday to my home country, Sudan, and my sister stayed in the UK with my dad. This holiday helped my mother destress and relax after everything we had discovered about my sister's health. While we were at a wedding celebration, my sister was taken to the hospital immediately for an emergency kidney transplant as a donor with a match was found for her. This cut our holiday short and we ended up coming back days earlier than planned. Fast forward a couple of years, my sister's health improved and she was only taking medication in order for her kidney to keep functioning. At this time, I had started primary school. I had quite a different primary school experience as I moved schools about six times before I entered secondary school, so I always had a few friends from each school I went to, but I was always having to be the "new girl" in each school I went to. Although I had made a lot of friends from each school I went to, I was picked on by the more "popular group" of individuals and I don't need to explain, I'm sure we all know what I'm talking about! I have a skin condition called eczema and I've had this since birth. I would frequently have flare ups, which were more predominant on my face. This became increasingly difficult to grow up with, especially going through primary and secondary school. My weight also influenced my time at secondary school. As a result of this bullying, my self-confidence has not always been the best compared to before when I had no issues with myself. As a teenager going through these obstacles in life, I never failed to keep a positive outlook on everything, even when life got tough.

One of the toughest moments of my life was when my father also had kidney problems as a result of his diabetes diagnosis. It didn't stop there, my father went through a period where he underwent a number of operations, one of the most significant being open-heart surgery. He required a pacemaker and a valve to open up his arteries. This occurred when I was 15 years old, so I was quite aware of the implications of his conditions. This started to affect my behaviour in school. Even though I tried to stay positive, I also couldn't help but be scared. I was the closest to my father as my mother was mostly with my sister, so naturally my father was the one who took care of me. He would take me to school, clubs, shopping with him. So, in a way, he was all I knew. My behaviour in school started to escalate, I was being given detention and put on reports. I was given a counsellor that I was required to visit once a week during school hours. From what I remember, I have always had a counsellor, from primary school through to college. Eventually, my father started improving and this made me feel hopeful, as I don't know what I would do if I lost him, and that moment in time made me feel how it would be like. This ordeal opened my eyes and made me realise that we should enjoy every day as it comes, appreciate our health and forever be grateful.

I was told this term by my counsellor, but I didn't really understand the idea until it was explained to me: "Glass Child". This is a term used for siblings of special needs children; the child with special needs requires extra attention from their parents so the sibling does not get noticed enough. This only recently resonated with me, and it all started to make sense. Some people may see this as something unfortunate, but I have learned to appreciate it. Maybe this was what I needed to become independent and get ready for the blessings I will experience in the future. With the trials I have been through, I have gone down each path having learnt a lesson and constantly improving myself. I have had times where I have had high highs and low lows, but I realise that I am a resilient individual and have bounced back from things life has thrown at me. Knowing this about myself at a young age is my biggest power. Knowing yourself is the best superpower to have. Nobody can take that away from you.

I went through the struggle of having to take care of somebody from a young age and I didn't really talk about it because I didn't think it was normal, nor did I think anyone would understand my struggle. But further research has showed me that quite a few young adults are going through the same thing, and I wanted them to know, you are not alone!

# OVERCOMING LIMITATIONS
## BY DOMINIKA CZAPLICKA

I moved to England from Poland when I was 13 years old with no knowledge of the language, culture or anything that awaited me. My family situation has never been easy, I moved abroad with just my mother, but our relationship has always been unstable. One thing I have always enjoyed is learning, and from a young age I told myself I wanted to achieve a university level education to be the first one in my close family. While achieving good grades in both school and college I found myself facing many challenges to reach my goal of attending university.

    I began to live independently at the age of 16, which came with the need to grow up a lot faster than others and take on more responsibilities. At that time, I still attended college and studied childcare and young years education. I can confidently say that it was hard, but also a learning experience that helped me get to where I am today. During this time I began to struggle with mental health issues and found it extremely difficult to ask for help as I was under the impression that I must be strong enough to deal with everything on my own. I feel that living independently at such a young age was difficult, sometimes lonely and sometimes brought some feelings of sadness, but I also believe it built my resilience and helped me with self-improvement. I graduated college with great results and rewards for my achievements. I received a university offer to continue my studies in childcare, however, as I was sofa surfing before getting my own flat, the lack of stability made my application for student funding quite difficult. In the end, after attending university for one and half weeks, I was unable to afford the studies and dropped out in order to find a full-time job to be able to support myself and cover all living expenses. I still had the ambition to return to education and complete my degree. It was a very hard decision and something that required big commitments.

I then had my own flat, a full-time job and cats. I also at that point in time received the diagnosis of anxiety and depression, and was very aware that change would be difficult for me. After many days of thinking and discussing my worries as well as ambitions with people close to me, I decided to apply to Sheffield Hallam University, but knew that childcare wasn't in fact my calling.

I've always liked working with numbers and problem solving, which made me think about a career in the finance world. When I turned 20, I saved up some money and decided to pack up my whole life, together with my two cats, and move to Sheffield after receiving an offer to study accounting and finance. Of course, as expected, change was difficult, and it didn't come without challenges. In those moments I felt scared and nervous, but also very excited about starting university and living in a new city.

The beginning of my university journey was in fact hard. I felt very alone and didn't know if I would meet new people who shared the same interests as me or even accept me for who I am. I was very afraid that I would spend my university years mostly alone, as parties and nights out weren't my definition of fun when moving to university. I soon realised how wrong I was about that. The opportunities to meet so many different people with a load of different perspectives, interests and views while at university is definitely possible, simply through communicating with others on your course, joining societies that fall into your interest to connect with people who are passionate about similar things, your housemates, or, in my case, neighbours who are fellow students who you simply click with. I can truly say I met some amazing people while at university who I hope to keep in my life forever and help me with the feelings of being alone and not understood by others.

I also became involved in societies. I joined the accounting and finance society committee as equality and diversity officer as it is something I am passionate about, to help create a space where everyone is welcome in the hope that I can make other people who feel as alone as I did at the beginning of my university journey feel like they belong and can connect with others. Making close friends with my course peers definitely made my university journey easier, it is great to have people you can talk to, trust and share the fun moments and the struggles we face while studying at university.

Through my university journey so far, I have already learnt so much. Not only education and knowledge of the finance industry, but also how many challenges I managed to overcome to get to the place I am now. Dealing with mental health issues and personal experiences impacted my university journey, making it hard at times, but also helped me to remember not to give up and to continue trying my hardest. If there is anything I hope for others to gain from my story it is that you should never limit yourself, always follow your ambition and remember that you are not alone.

I wanted to share my story with others in the hope that it could help somebody considering attending university while feeling alone and unsure of where they belong. I've always thought of university level education as an entirely personal choice. We must attend school, however, carrying on your education and choosing a particular career is our own option. University is hard and requires commitment and willingness to self-study and gain knowledge about your chosen career industry and practices, and with additional challenges faced along the university journey it can be difficult to navigate it. It might require some extra hard work and is sometimes filled with negative feelings. In those times I think it is important to remember to take care of ourselves and our minds. I personally recommend lemon tea and watching your comfort show.

In this chapter I also wanted to let people know that your battle with mental health doesn't have to be fought alone. Anyone experiencing those struggles know that our brains have the ability to make us believe many things about ourselves and world around us, to make us feel alone and scared to ask for help. When joining Sheffield Hallam University, I soon found out about so many great resources and help available to meet my individual needs. I found support for many different struggles, not only mental health but also with personal situations, such as my experience of being estranged from my parents, which can be very difficult for many students. There are some amazing teams of people who really made the effort to understand me and offer as much help as possible to make my time at university easier. Asking for help can be very difficult and nobody should ever feel like they're less when needing that additional help.

# THE UNTOLD STORY OF MENTORSHIP
## BY FAITH OGALA

The motivation behind sharing my mentorship story with the reader stems from the belief that everyone, regardless of age or background, can benefit from the transformative power of mentorship. My journey is a testament to the untold story behind personal and professional development – the silent force that propels individuals to greater heights. I want to shed light on the significance of mentorship, breaking down the misconception that it is only for beginners or those early in their careers.

In sharing my story, I hope the reader takes away the understanding that mentorship is a lifelong journey. It is not confined to a specific stage of one's career but evolves and adapts to the changing landscapes of life. The mentor-mentee relationship is a dynamic force that can propel individuals forward, providing the necessary support, guidance, and encouragement to navigate personal and professional life complexities. The central themes of resilience, adaptability, and the transformative power of mentorship are interwoven throughout my narrative. I want the reader to recognise that mentorship is not merely about receiving advice on career choices but extends to building character, instilling discipline, and fostering adaptability. The profound impact of genuine guidance can shape not only one's career but also one's entire outlook on life.

Moreover, I hope the reader understands that mentorship is a reciprocal relationship. While mentors offer guidance, mentees bring their unique perspectives, energy, and enthusiasm. It is a collaborative journey where both parties contribute to each other's growth, fostering an environment of continuous learning and development. In the broader context, I aspire for the reader to appreciate the significance of mentorship in the professional realm. Every success story, including mine, has a mentor behind it – someone who believed in the mentee's potential and invested time and effort in their growth. This recognition is vital for individuals and organisations alike, emphasising the role of mentorship in shaping the success and sustainability of industries.

From college to my career and application for my PhD, I've been fortunate to have mentors who've guided me every step of the way. Navigating the intricate landscape of academia and career development in the UK posed a formidable challenge due to my lack of prior experience. Despite these hurdles, the unwavering support and mentorship from Dr. Isaac, Dr. Ifeoma and Dr Francis became a beacon of guidance in my journey. Their encouragement helped me surmount obstacles and led me to a defining moment when I embraced the ASPIRE programme. The pivotal moment in my journey was when I was introduced to the ASPIRE programme through my mentors and had the opportunity to connect with scholars from the first cohort. Their experiences and the mentorship of my lecturers inspired me to pursue the programme, setting the stage for a transformative journey.

Under their tutelage, I gained insights and a reservoir of resilience to confront the complexities of professional life. During my master's programme, I embarked on a transformative journey with these mentors who shaped my career. We've had meetings stretching into midnight, with them even serving as my referees during crucial phases like my application for a Job and PhD. Their wealth of experience in my field was invaluable, providing insights fuelling my passion and determination. Collaborative virtual meetings on Teams were not just routine discussions; they involved detailed reports, mock interviews and strategic planning sessions. These mentors motivated me to succeed and opened a spectrum of career opportunities, instilling a sense of seriousness and focus, proving that even busy individuals can profoundly impact one's trajectory. They motivate me to be successful, empower me to make decisions and make me want to improve. Their unwavering belief in me was exemplified when they ensured my participation at the International Festival of Public Health conference at the University of Manchester, guiding me to present my work and in winning the Santander bank scholarship. This gesture reinforced their commitment and belief in my potential.

Their support has been instrumental in my academic achievements and professional growth. The connection with these mentors was a game-changer, echoing the sentiment that everything changes when the right person comes along. The mentorship went beyond mere career advice; it was a transformative experience that breathed life into my professional journey. I discovered that no matter how many years you have spent in the industry, you are never too old to benefit from mentorship.

Throughout my journey, I have encountered numerous valuable lessons that have shaped my perspective and approach to life. One of the most significant lessons I have learned is the importance of resilience. Life is rarely a smooth ride, and setbacks are inevitable. Resilience allows us to bounce back from adversity, learn from our mistakes, and grow stronger. Another crucial lesson is the significance of building a solid support system. Surrounding oneself with mentors, friends, and loved ones who believe in our potential and provide guidance is essential for personal and professional growth. The journey has also taught me the power of adaptation and flexibility. Being open to change and embracing new opportunities has led to unexpected and transformative experiences. These lessons have profoundly influenced my mindset and continue to guide me on my path.

Overcoming challenges and embracing opportunities have been fundamental to my personal and professional growth. It is through adversity that we discover our true strength and resilience. I have faced numerous challenges throughout my journey, from periods of self-doubt to navigating complex work situations. Each challenge has presented an opportunity for growth and learning. By persevering through difficult times, I have developed new skills, gained confidence in my abilities, and expanded my knowledge. Embracing opportunities, big and small, has allowed me to step out of my comfort zone and discover hidden talents. Whether taking on a leadership role or seizing a chance to travel for work, each opportunity has enriched my journey and contributed to my overall development. I have driven a meaningful path filled with growth and fulfilment by facing challenges head-on and embracing opportunities.

My mentorship journey is more than a personal reflection; it is a testament to the enduring value of mentorship throughout one's career. I hope the reader recognises the untold story of mentorship goes beyond professional milestones, reaching the core of personal growth, resilience, and the shared human experience of overcoming challenges. Embracing mentorship is not a one-time event but a continuous journey that spans a lifetime, enriching both the mentor and the mentee.

Mentorship has guided my life, profoundly shaping my resilience, character, and career trajectory. Embarking on my journey within the embrace of a supportive Christian family set the cornerstone for my values and beliefs, with my parents' unwavering dedication and involvement infusing me with a profound sense of confidence and determination. However, as the chapters of my life unfolded in the professional realm, the unpredictable nature of existence presented a series of formidable challenges. The lack of experiential wisdom in this new environment became apparent, from navigating personal hardships to overcoming academic hurdles. Each trial, though arduous, etched its mark on my evolving identity. Amidst these trials, the defining moments cast the longest shadows, leaving an indelible mark on the intricate tapestry of my journey.

The themes of resilience, adaptability, and the transformative power of mentorship are central to my story. Navigating the challenges of being a student required me to yield to the advice of my mentors, be sincere in seeking their guidance, and keep them informed of my progress. Their mentorship impacted my student journey and contributed to my academic achievements, including receiving the MSc

Public Health postgraduate prize.

Throughout my student journey, I have embraced the guidance of my mentors and remained sincere in dealing with personal experiences. This approach has allowed me to develop as a disciplined, adaptable, and resilient individual, contributing to my academic accomplishments and professional endeavours.

My journey as a Hallam Help administrator and a Culture Connect mentor sharpened my teamwork and collaboration skills. It nurtured my communication and cultural awareness, proving pivotal for my professional development. This foundation and the transformative power of effective teamwork experienced during my student assessments and projects have shaped my growth and learning.

The impact of mentorship extends beyond personal growth, as evidenced by the connections and moments shared with peers during team assessments. The right mentor can change everything, providing the guidance and support needed to thrive in one's career. Every success story is often rooted in the influence of a fantastic mentor whose advice and encouragement serve as the magic ingredient for professional growth. Behind the facade of personal achievements and professional milestones lies the untold story of mentorship – the silent force that propels individuals to greater heights. It's the mentor who nudges you forward when you're on the brink of retreat, imparts wisdom that transcends textbooks, and the ally who stands by you when the journey gets tough.

I aim to evoke the themes of resilience, growth, and the profound impact of genuine guidance. The narrative is a testament to the power of mentorship, showcasing that, even in a world that often celebrates self-sufficiency, the presence of a mentor can be the magic ingredient that propels a career to unprecedented heights. The mentorship I have received has been a driving force in my personal and professional development. Behind every success story is a fantastic mentor, and I am grateful for the guidance and support I have received throughout my journey.

Not every mentorship story is conventional, and the age or background of a mentor is not a limiting factor. A mentor can open new career opportunities and provide the necessary push for continued growth. A mentor's tough yet fair approach can lead to significant professional development, regardless of one's years of experience.

Looking back on my journey, I am grateful for every experience that has shaped me into who I am today. Each step has been a valuable lesson from the highs to the lows. I have learned the importance of perseverance, self-reflection, and the power of embracing change. My journey reminds me of the importance of staying true to myself and following my passions. It taught me to trust the process and believe in my abilities, even in adversity. Every hurdle and triumph have contributed to my growth, and I am forever grateful for the opportunities that have come my way.

If I could offer advice to my 16-year-old self, there is a lot to say to her; it would be to embrace the unknown and fearlessly pursue her dreams. Uncertainty often clouds our judgement at that age, and societal expectations can steer us away from our true passions. I would tell my younger self to listen to her intuition, even when it contradicts popular opinion. I would urge her to take risks, explore various paths, and never let the fear of failure hold her back. By acknowledging that failure is a natural part of growth, my 16-year-old self would learn to see every setback as an opportunity for learning and development. Embracing this mindset would lead to a more fulfilling and authentic journey. It would also be helpful to embrace mentorship early on. I would encourage my younger self to seek guidance, be open to learning from others, and understand that the path to success is often paved with the wisdom shared by those who have walked similar roads. Mentorship is not a sign of weakness but a testament to the strength gained through shared experiences and insights.

Mentorship has transformed my career pathway, shaping my resilience, character, and professional growth. The impact of mentorship is far-reaching, and I am a testament to the profound influence of dedicated mentors in guiding and shaping one's career trajectory. A famous saying aptly puts it: "You are never too old to be mentored," emphasising the enduring value of mentorship in every stage of one's career journey and life.

# BE MINDFUL OF YOUR INNER STRENGTH
## BY FATIMAH ADESANYA

I chased a twist of multiple life goals at the same time which made me think I do things larger than myself. Even when I was anxious and uncertain, I challenged myself to seek more for my career progression, embraced a better attitude, and remained in the lives of those who matter to me most. Now I look back to see how I got my inner strength and vigour to try and try again. I see an unending quest for knowledge, having a good family, and finding a purposeful life in me and all that I can control. I hope my journey inspires and drives others who have a burning desire to rebound and progress.

## Career growth, family life & survival

I had a good beginning, graduating with good grades at the right time from the University of Lagos, Nigeria. Everything almost went perfectly as I got my first job six months after my first-degree graduation. My career started as an audit trainee in a mid-tier audit firm in Lagos, the third most populous city in Africa. At that point, it didn't matter whether I wanted to be a Chartered Accountant or not, all I wanted was to start a professional job.

I also wanted to have a master's degree and a Ph.D. at some point in life, but I didn't know when and how. This was a childhood aspiration. At the same time, I looked forward to having a happy home with beautiful children. I just thought everything was okay to desire as it makes life worthwhile, busy, and bustling. As I found myself amid all my life goals, life happened, and challenges struck more and more.

To progress in my job, I had to complete my accountancy professional exams within three years, but this did not happen as planned. Though I managed to obtain a master's degree in economics exactly a year into my job, unfortunately, it did not give me the progression I desired in my place of work or provide me with a new job offer. So, I went further to start an MPhil/PhD programme which I later abandoned. Maybe this academic pursuit was too pushy or unplanned, but I leave you to reason along with me as I narrate my story.

Throughout this time, I had started my family, enjoying marital bliss with a little daughter to nurture and care for. Due to several failed attempts at exams, I remained in the same job position for nine years. It was a huge loss for me as my finances shrank due to a delayed job promotion despite my hard work and resilience. And of course, my expenses grew bigger as I spent money to retake exams and pay other bills.

Though these circumstances made my colleagues and managers think less of me, at times despondent and inept, I continued to articulate and take responsibility for tasks allocated to me. I simply carried on with what made me happy. I would read academic articles and follow political and business news. If I fail in one field, I will be informed and at least have a say in other areas.

## Breaking my records

All these came to me as loads of responsibilities that almost tore me apart. I couldn't find a new job or change my career; I needed money to pay for my tuition or get new training if a career change was to become an option. I endured a pressured working environment that made me feel less than myself. I remember my senior partner making doubtful comments about how long it would take me to pass and whether it would ever happen. The only thing that kept me going was a supportive family who understood how much of a toll these conditions were taking on me. Nothing changed until my ninth year on the job and just when I started another maternity leave. That year was significant and defined me in many ways.

It was unimaginable that I could write and pass three papers at once while nursing my second baby who was only a few weeks old. When the results were released, the firm made it official, I thought it was an accident because I had failed and re-written papers but never passed under less complex conditions. I made it under the greatest of pressure and then looked back to see determination, self-assurance, and self-definition. I had gone through nine years of heavy emotional stress, unforgiving sacrifices, and disappointments affecting me and my family.

Now, those days' struggles I endured have become the good old days I laugh about today! My promotion came next after my results were announced, but I was ready to move on to another job or possibly start a new life elsewhere. Consolably, I changed my job twice within the next two years in the city of Lagos. In my last job, I worked as a finance manager at an award-winning dry fruit processing company where I learned new great skills that helped later.

## Still chasing my dreams in a new land

A whole lot of factors were responsible for my relocation decision – seeking a better life and developing a well-rounded personality. I was not sure whether I would like to pay the price of getting things right again. In my private moments, I thought I may have missed it, and why I decided to relocate. I reflected on my patchy beginnings; how setting priorities, asking for support, time management, information gathering, and purposeful relationships had allowed me to stay focused and see me through my tough career progress.

I started another master's degree in accounting and finance at Sheffield Hallam University with limited resources to support my family's living costs. Then another period of struggling began again. One would expect that I could secure a good part-time job soon, but it had never been easy for international students to settle, and more challenging for students with families. At times I asked myself if this was a life trap to keep studying as I hadn't made enough money from my hard work and education.

It would have been easy to carry on with low-skill jobs, but they would not have fulfilled my dreams of becoming me. So, I kept on applying for part-time jobs until I got a stroke of luck on charityjob.co.uk. I describe this as "sheer luck" again; because many professional migrants struggled to secure decent jobs in the UK due to racial disharmony, poor social networks, and more.

I worked as a financial consultant on a part-time contract job at a charity organisation located in Manchester. I owe this opportunity to my 10 years of bitter working experience which I leveraged in an entirely new space. Gradually, I was able to pay more bills, and life became easier as I integrated into the system.

I also volunteered on several projects and made purposeful relationships with my new friends and senior colleagues. Now, I am on the board of a multi-academy trust and a treasurer of a charity for young minoritised people. I hope to do more, but also earn more money for my skills and experience. My family settled well in our new city and life has started moving well.

Looking ahead, I agree that not all circumstances are wasteful, but its learnings may serve us when we need it most. The most challenging parts of our lives are most times intended to shape and strengthen our values and personality. Though it may be seen as a long string of failures, it's more than bracing us for our future goals and aspirations.

## My new adventure

If I had been told that I would still chase more dreams in academia, I would doubt it. I had to abandon it about 10 years ago. As I was completing my dissertation, a PhD-GTA position was advertised, and I gave it an attempt. Although the application deadline was close to my dissertation submission, I tirelessly put together a proposal on a research topic funded by the university. I think my childhood aspiration to pursue a Ph.D. had not left me and this pushed me further.

I did my best on the proposal and thankfully I was shortlisted for an interview. Here, the value of the relationships I made during my 15-month master's programme became more meaningful. I got enormous support from senior colleagues and great mentors who arranged a series of mock interviews for me. I would suggest it is always good to seek help because those who will support you need your consent too.

I did my interview with a six-member panel with tough questions on academics, personalities, and career prospects. I waited eagerly for the results. Just like every interview, I could not tell what the outcome could be. At times success comes when it's most uncertain, or as one just takes what life throws back at you. The great news is that I got the position, and I am now a doctoral student who will be starting a career in higher education at Sheffield Hallam University.

## Times and reflections

My story would have been different if I had planned my life goals as step-by-step events. Well, I am not sure if I was over-ambitious, but I am certain of what I want out of life. I did not seek help when I should have, or I was confused about having too many hats on. I later became self-aware and embraced my life through resilience and determination. I am always learning and developing myself to be my very best. In all of this, I have grown and endured tough times enough to adapt to anywhere I find myself. For everyone going through life, either in career pursuits, relocation hurdles or as a defined person, I encourage you to find life, rebound, and progress. Good luck!

# BEYOND BOUNDARIES: NAVIGATING CHALLENGES, DEFYING NORMS AND INSPIRING SUCCESS

## BY GLADYS AWOLOWO

Life's challenges, particularly my upbringing in the Northern part of my home country where cultural and religious norms discouraged the education of girls, posed significant hurdles. Despite the prevailing beliefs, my parents remained unwavering in their determination to provide a university education for all their children. In the face of societal norms, my determination and resilience propelled me through the completion of my first degree.

Being guided by a relatable role model has significantly influenced my present identity and the person I am evolving into. The combination of my university education and exposure through travels has not only shaped my worldview but has also ignited a profound desire to positively influence and impact others. The influential figures in my life, such as Professor Nigel Garrow and others, have been instrumental in inspiring me to aim for greater accomplishments, altering the trajectory of both my life and career. Now, with newfound aspirations, I am eager to embark on a PhD journey, envisioning a future in academia with the ultimate goal of becoming a professor.

However, the journey did not conclude there. In a culture where women are expected to prioritise marriage and motherhood over furthering their education, I, with the support and motivation from my husband and kids, defied these expectations. I pursued and completed a master's degree at Sheffield Hallam University, an experience that proved to be transformative. Now, with the momentum gained, I am aspiring to delve into a doctoral study in the near future.

My narrative echoes themes of determination, resilience, and the profound impact that supportive individuals can have on one's achievements. It serves as a testament to the idea that with tenacity and a supportive network, one can overcome societal expectations and achieve one's aspirations.

Failures of the past, the fear of 'I can't succeed', and finally 'making it' are moments that have impacted me and slowed me down; it took a few years in between going for my degree and master's, but because of the determination of wanting to improve myself every day and socialising through learning and wanting to learn new things shaped and impacted who I am today.

First, I want you to be determined and always tell yourself you can make it and not settle for less; never think you are the second best; you are always the first. I always tell my family that I want my 10-year-old past self to be proud of who she has become now, and I want my future self to look back and pat myself on the back and say, well done, you did it. As a girl child who is not supposed to go to school, I did it till this point. I want my husband to say to himself proudly: 'that's my wife'. Finally, I want my kids to be proud of their mum growing up. I even encouraged my mum to go to school because she got married at a young age and did not have the opportunity. I did not want to end up the same, which is part of what shaped who I am today; seeing how determined I was, my mum also went back to study and graduated at 50+ years, and I was one of the people who encouraged her, and I keep telling her how proud I am.

I want my kids to be proud of me, and I also want them to see me as their role model; if I achieve a greater height, chances are they will also one day want to be like their mum. Hopefully, one day. So, I would like you to keep going too. It might not be an easy road, and you may face challenges, but surrounding yourself with the right people, people further along and successful that you can model your life after, will raise you up.

There are lots of challenges I have faced personally, such as getting married. As I have said earlier, I could have just decided that you know what, that is it for me. I will stop there and look after my family, but no, I kept pushing to where I am today. Also, during my master's degree, the lecture times were always very early in the morning, and assessments were due for submission at the same time, group meetings and lots of activities, such as being the course rep and representing my class in meetings. This was so much of a challenge but I was able to pull through it all. It was not easy going to lectures and looking after a young family; sometimes, when I got back from 6pm lectures, I dropped my bag in the lounge and went into the kitchen to cook till I went to bed; after seeing to the kids. It was not an easy journey, but was it worth it? The answer is YES! What kept me going then was the end goal of wanting to better myself and achieve a greater height. I was so happy and proud of myself when I was awarded my master's degree last November in 2023. It made my heart full.

My time at Hallam has been perfect, and they were so supportive. I have gained lots of skills and have been able to meet new people from various countries and learn about other cultures, such as Hungary, Pakistan, India, Nigeria, and Britain. The lecturers were very helpful in terms of the lectures and making sure we had academic advisor meetings in case we were struggling academically.

Hallam has helped me gain good time management skills where I was able to manage my time specifically in the process of doing my assessment and meeting deadlines, which is an excellent transferable skill into any industry.

I was also able to join the Achieve programme, which was an intensive programme that helped with how to write a CV, questions to expect when going for an interview, etc.

One of my best memories is of the excellent practicals we used to attend in level 12 of Owen building, where we got to do apply practical elements of what we had been taught, with great help from the kitchen staff. The kitchen is one of the best and neatest kitchens I have seen so far, and I have learnt lots of great things from them. Also, I like that during our intervention classes, we could use actual participants for our samples, which made me learn quickly, and all the equipment was up-to-date and sophisticated, which I remember seeing in hospitals and some great companies.

I also got great support from the SSA Student support advisor who helped me immensely through her understanding of my circumstances during and after my exam . My mum was involved in a ghastly accident just the week of my exam period, which really affected my preparation, and the concern impacted my result negatively. I was so let down and depressed and didn't know what to do until the result came out, and it was not what I was expecting. My module leader told me to contact the SSA to find out if something could be done. We had several meetings with her until I started clearing my exam. The resit date for the exam on one of my modules had passed, but my SSA was able to help. Even though I was preparing to re-register for the module, my SSA hadn't heard about my excruciating circumstances, but realised it was genuine and signposted me to where to get further help. I was able to retake the exam, and I was successful. Now I could graduate with my course mates. I was delighted and grateful for the opportunity to do the exam and pass without disappointing my SSA.

I have been to some other universities, but I haven't seen such a well-put-together graduation ceremony as the one at Hallam University. It was hosted in a great space and the crowds were treated to a lovely ceremony, and I was part of the graduating student cohort.

I think about a lot of things that I feel I should write down to help someone out there. I never gave up, so you should never give up. Keep trying and you will get there, no matter your age, young or old, if you don't help yourself no one will. If I can do it with the challenges life has thrown my way, I believe you can do it too. I hope this chapter will help you feel you can reach the top no matter your background, your race, your gender, your status, or whatever you are going through. Bad days and times don't last forever. Slow and steady wins the race; do not compare yourself with others; it is not a competition. Believe in yourself and self-reflect frequently. Thank you for reading my story; write your own unique story because you are who you are.

# TAKE THE RISK
## BY JAMES V. R. OLDERSHAW

In sharing my story and experiences, my aim is to provide inspiration to individuals still navigating their next steps. This is particularly directed towards those who might think they've missed the opportunity to pursue a university education or feel that their on-paper representation falls short.

I stand as an example, and this is my story.

Having spent most of my childhood in a small village in Portugal, at the age of 13, I uprooted my life. I left behind all that was familiar, trading the quiet countryside of my hometown for the diverse cityscape of London. This move marked the start of a new chapter in my life and my unconventional academic journey. After settling into school life, my first significant hurdle arose when I failed maths - a setback that, at the time, felt like the end of the world. Undeterred, I decided to apply myself in college, where I not only achieved a distinction and two merits in my Business BTEC Level 3 diploma but also faced the challenge of retaking my maths GCSE.

Yet, life's circumstances led me to decide against pursuing a university education, a choice that later left me with the feeling of missed opportunities. Opting for a different path, I entered the working world, securing a position with a proprietary trading firm. Like many young adults completing their education, the excitement of receiving my first pay cheque gave me a taste of financial independence. The idea of earning and managing my own money and the freedom to spend it as I saw fit, significantly influenced my decision-making process. At that point in time, the prospect of continuing to earn money held a greater appeal to me than the pursuit of higher education. Over the following three years I held various jobs while concurrently dedicating time to my hobby and passion – trading. In my position as a night concierge, I often found quiet late hours to focus on my trading, deepening my interest and ultimately influencing my decision to pursue a career as a professional trader. However, at the age of 21, surrounded by friends in graduation gowns, I couldn't help but feel as though I had missed my chance. A conversation with a close friend sparked the idea of enrolling in a one-year master's course. Fuelled by my passion for trading, I realised that a professional path in this field necessitated relevant qualifications in the trading and finance sector. Despite apprehensions about being accepted due to my somewhat unconventional academic background, I decided to embrace the risk and apply, recognising that I had nothing to lose.

    I applied to three universities and proactively tracked down and reached out to course directors, expressing my enthusiasm, and detailing my unique situation through email. The response was positive from one of the universities, leading to an interview with the course leader, Damion Taylor. A time and date were set up for a phone conversation in order for Damion to discuss my motivations and skillset and was a chance for me to settle any concerns he might have had. Whilst some concerns regarding my academic background were raised, the phone call allowed me to showcase my passion and practical trading experiences. I also gained a deeper insight into the program regarding the modules, how I would be assessed, and the skill set required in order to excel.

Following my initial phone interview with Mr Taylor, I was asked to speak to the Global Head of Professional Trader Qualifications at OSTC who worked in partnership with the university on the MSc in Global Financial Trading. Subsequently, I had an in-depth conversation with Robert Russell which allowed me to delve much deeper into my experiences and motivations, and demonstrate a comprehensive understanding of markets, derivatives, and trading. This helped strengthen my candidacy. Despite initial reservations, the recommendation for my admission was made by Mr Russell. A few weeks later I eagerly received a call from Damion Taylor who extended an exceptional offer to join the first cohort of the MSc in Global Financial Trading. Ecstatic, I accepted the offer and prepared for the challenges ahead, resigning from my current job and organising my finances and accommodation.

Acknowledging the pressures ahead and the expectation to work exceptionally hard, given the risk taken in accepting me onto the course, I faced initial struggles. Having never produced written work to university standards, I found myself in a disadvantaged position compared to my peers, all of whom had at least three years of university study under their belts. Despite barely passing my first assignment, scraping the bare minimum required for a pass mark, my strong-willed and motivated nature compelled me to put in extra effort to prove to both myself and the university that I could excel in the programme. I dedicated time to reading journal articles, familiarising myself with proper essay structure and improving my referencing skills. This dedication transformed my grade, turning them from pass to distinction. Determined to maintain my excellent grades, I continued to work even harder. Writing a master's level dissertation without prior university experience presented significant challenges, requiring me to navigate complex research methodologies. The lack of a foundational understanding in academic writing added an extra layer of difficulty, as I had to quickly grasp new concepts and report-style structure.

Despite these hurdles, the experience served as a significant learning curve, highlighting the resilience needed to overcome unfamiliar academic terrain and successfully complete my dissertation. Given my passion for the subject, assignments gradually become second nature to me. I am proud to say I graduated top of my class with a distinction, achieving this remarkable feat without possessing an undergraduate degree or A-levels. Another significant achievement was my dissertation which was arguably the most demanding part of the whole MSc program. Choosing my dissertation topic and refining a compelling research question was a time-consuming process, involving careful consideration to pinpoint a specific area of interest. At the time, I often felt the pressures of the time constraints, feeling as though perhaps I had bitten off more than I could chew. However, after few late nights and early mornings in the library coupled with sheer determination, I submitted a dissertation to be proud of. I was ecstatic to learn that I was awarded 78% for my dissertation which greatly contributed to achieving a distinction overall for my master's.

Reflecting on my journey, If I could offer my unsure sixteen-year-old self some advice, it would be to take the risk as what is the worst that can happen? Perhaps you will be told 'no', but you will never know if you do not push yourself to take the chance to find out. I would also say to be personable and have lots of charisma, as this will help you to connect with people and the more you network the more doors will open for you. Remember it's not always what you know, sometimes it's who you know. Regardless of your experiences and background always be confident in the value you bring to the table and whether people can see the potential in you or not, you know yourself best so keep trying and eventually you will get to where you want to go.

Since finishing university, I am now faced with the next life hurdle like many other graduates, entering the world of work and securing the right position. My university experience has equipped me with a polished CV, connections from my journey and sheer enthusiasm. Currently, I am actively applying for positions in at investment banks, hedge funds and commodity trading houses and very much look forward to the challenges that lie ahead.

I hope my journey serves as an inspiration, demonstrating that perseverance and determination can overcome perceived barriers to success. If my story resonates with you, remember that even if you believe certain opportunities are not accessible because you haven't taken the 'traditional' route, you can still achieve them too.

# BREAKING CYCLES
## BY KHAYA WINFIELD

If there was one thing I could tell my younger self, it's that often in life, you'll notice behaviours come and go in cycles. We're given two choices: to either repeat the cycle or break it. The latter is not always as easy as it sounds. To do this, you must constantly show up for yourself, proving to yourself that you are more than just your experiences, that you can overcome your circumstances.

To begin, let me tell you a bit about myself. The environment I grew up in could often be described as difficult, chaotic, unkind and often void of suitable role models.

When I was younger, I was fortunate enough to be surrounded by people who often talked about wealth and encouraged academic success; however, I did not feel I fit the criteria for such success. I noticed that the people I met who were advocating for these things grew up in different circumstances, many from high-end, wealthy backgrounds, often unable to relate to events that I felt could hinder my success. It was like I was trying to win a race that had already been fixed against me.

I knew that if I wanted to achieve success, it would mean I would have to work harder and smarter than those around me. I would have to constantly prove myself. There was one thing I realised about my circumstances though, which you could almost call an advantage; my motivation to succeed was so much stronger. It was a need, not a want. I needed better for myself and those around me.

Some of these experiences came from my ethnicity and sexuality. Growing up in a small town, it was rare that I would find anyone I could relate to who had achieved what I wanted to achieve. There was a lack of people of colour, and throughout my childhood, I experienced more hate than I saw happen to others. However, it took me a while to try and piece together why. I would witness events that made me feel as if people like me were less than human, whether these were degrading comments, slurs, or watching people with the same sexuality being verbally or physically abused. Eventually, this led to deep feelings of isolation, damaging self-esteem, and hindered motivation and growth.

Ever since I was younger, a large part of my childhood was focused on my younger sister. The struggle of trying to support someone at such a young age became evident as I grew older, having to take on more responsibilities in my own life and in someone else's. Nevertheless, I would show up at every school meeting, take her everywhere she needed to be, and make sure she always knew I would be there for her. Having experienced challenging circumstances myself, I knew how difficult things may be for her, and I wanted her to know she would not be alone, finding comfort in the knowledge that I had the ability to help and make a difference in her life. However, attempting to guide someone through circumstances you yourself have not yet overcome can be extremely challenging and next to impossible.

Nevertheless, the more difficult your circumstances, the greater your motivation to overcome them can be.

One of the main issues I experienced that hindered my success was periods of stagnancy and inaction. The huge difference I found between staying where I was and progressing in life was having a belief that there was somewhere to go. Growing up, it was easy to compare myself to others, to see only what our lives were lacking. Compared to the people I was surrounded with, we often had less. Less money, less support, and less of a community. Often being outcast from certain circles due to people's lack of understanding. However, at the time, I could not see the reasoning behind this, and it's easy to hate those that you don't understand.

The most helpful thing I could do was envision not only a better life for myself but also for others. The difficult part was believing that such a thing was achievable. For me, this was one of the hardest obstacles to overcome. Often, when I reached out for support, I was met with responses such as, 'You should be grateful things aren't worse,' and 'You should focus more on accepting things than fighting for change.' I was repeatedly told change wasn't possible or deserved. Being constantly told these statements at a young age can be detrimental; it often becomes your own narrative.

Believing differently is often extremely difficult, especially when witnessing a system, you're taught to believe in constantly damaging people that you care for. This happened in countless circumstances; however, a major experience is one regarding my younger brother. He has a disability called Down syndrome, and throughout his life, it has been a constant fight to try and get him the support and education he needs, as many people see him only as his disability, not acknowledging him as the individual he is. He is instead marginalised, with his own capabilities and potential overlooked, replaced with prejudice and preconceived beliefs.

My life began to change when I no longer accepted things for the way they were and decided that I would rather spend my time fighting for better than accepting that was all there was. Some of the most impactful pieces of advice I've heard are to become the designer of your world, not just the consumer of it, and that all of us can live better than we are right now. After watching people around me, constantly repeating negative cycles that not only damaged themselves but also others, I decided that if there was no better way, then we needed to make one.

For me, freedom from these cycles came from education. Not typical academic education, but by educating myself on the causes and symptoms of such behavioural and mental cycles. Once I'd made the decision to commit myself to change, I believed the way to be able to do this was through knowledge. I began to teach myself about the reasoning behind others' perspectives, finding a passion for learning about different behaviours, cultures, philosophies, and beliefs. This helped me gain a greater perspective on life that allowed me to become open to learning and growth. Out of everything I studied, the most useful thing I learnt was the psychology behind habits. Applying this to myself allowed me to begin to see undeniable changes I previously believed were unachievable.

My journey to this point had not been a constantly positive one but rather one with constant ups and downs. Every time I achieved something for myself, getting one step closer to the life I wanted, to affirm the belief that better existed. It proved I was capable of achieving it.

As I learnt how to cope better and better with my situations, every problem that was thrown at me seemed to be slightly less difficult, and every negative comment and action became slightly less impactful. The problems that couldn't be solved became evermore easy to accept. Every time I would find myself falling back into bad habits, I would remind myself of a time I had come out of them and broken the cycle. Whether this was negative thought patterns, beliefs, or behaviours, the principle was the same.

One of the most useful things I learnt was that the best way to see change was to make it. In order to move forward, it was essential for me to start at the building blocks. The first step was recognising what kept me from growing, then finding a way to overcome it. For me, this was negative thought patterns and environments. Most of my direction came from gaining a deeper understanding of the people and situations that affected me. Learning that people's negative reactions are often just a reflection of their own inner mental states and experiences helped me to make peace with things that were holding me back. It took away the 'personal' aspect of people's actions and the constant questioning as to why they behaved the way they did. These things were eventually replaced with clarity, self-confidence, and self-determination. If people's behaviours had been learnt, they could also be unlearnt. This statement gave me a sense of belief that things do not always have to be the way they have been and applying it to myself allowed me to adapt to my situations instead of resisting them.

If I could summarise the most useful thing I've learnt, it would be to accept, adapt, and overcome instead of to hate, resist, and avoid. These qualities create and inspire change. They were not easy to learn, but they were the key building blocks in helping me reach my goals and ambitions and get to the place I am today.

# PERSEVERING TO ACHIEVE
## BY MARIAM OLUWATOYIN ADEBOYE

My journey of life has navigated many challenges, sometimes rewarded with sweet memories after the toughest of times. Sharing a part of my story will encourage anyone reading it to understand never to give up on themselves because there are always better days ahead of every wait and struggle. I cannot write everything in this chapter, but here is a glimpse.

After secondary school, I experienced a long delay getting into university. Although there was a long waiting time, I used it to learn new skills, I enrolled for the A level programme, and I battled a severe illness for about two years that nearly took my life. I could not sit my A level final exam, but I went back after my set had graduated to sit mine. Glory to God Almighty, I survived it and life continued. The wait for the university admission felt endless, I became confused and lost hope, leading to low self-esteem and lack of confidence, but the admission came at the last minute to put a smile on my face. I was admitted at the University of Ilorin to study Plant Biology.

After graduation, a new life journey began. I was extremely happy to have made it to graduation despite the long wait and my health challenges. My mum travelled to Ilorin to celebrate with me. She could not hold her joy seeing me graduate because she had witnessed my pain and struggles through life during and after my health challenges. I proceeded to my National Youth Service Corp (NYSC), a one-year service programme in Nigeria every graduate does after university to serve the country. I planned to go for a master's programme after NYSC, but financial consideration led me to seek a job first. I did not get one, and I faced challenges in job hunting. After NYSC, I travelled back home to continue my job hunting. About a month after, I went back to the state where I served to source for a job. I had in mind, I would get a job and retain my rented apartment to continue life there, but had a plan that if I did not, I would go to my aunty in another state for job hunting before going back home.

When I got to my aunty, we tried together in search of a job, but I did not have one before my mum called saying I should come home because a friend of hers said she could assist me with getting a job. The following week I travelled back home. I had the plan to work on the vocational skills I learnt during NYSC, leather work and food processing to start a business whilst I continued to apply for jobs in case the job my mum's friend promised did not work out. When I got home, I did not get the promised job and my plan did not go well with the businesses.

I went back to my casual marketing research job I used to do as a recruiter and interviewer before I was admitted in the university, I enrolled myself onto caregiving training due to my interest in healthcare, and I got involved in network marketing that deals with organic products and also started home improvement and a kitchen gadgets business online. I went into the field to interview people house to house sometimes in the rain or scorching sun to meet my target. I went along with my products from the network marketing company to sell. It caused lots of struggles for me. Sometimes I did not get to eat before setting off for the field work because I had lost my appetite due to stress. Although I struggled with eating food and choice of food, I thought doing so much would help me get enough to take care of myself and have a little savings. Unfortunately, that was not the case. The job hunting was continuing on the side. I went to various recruiting companies with my CV and attended their job searching webinars, but none were positive. I went to companies directly and in search of a job, but no opportunities were found. There were a lot of rejections with comments that were not encouraging.

After one and a half years I eventually secured a role as an administrative assistant through a friend's recommendation. Although it was a distance, and the pay was not as expected to cover transport and have good savings, I did not mind. All I wanted was a job to have a stable monthly income at that time. Eight months into the job the COVID-19 pandemic hit, and we were asked to stay at home following the government announcement. Although we continued work remotely it became boring. I continued with my personal businesses as the salary was not sufficient and my savings dwindled. I engaged with online webinars and trainings during the lockdown. After the lockdown, I was not called back to work. I found myself back on the job market. I felt relaxed when I got my first job, instead of hopping my game to keep applying since I have gained corporate experience, but I did not. So, I had to start all over again after I lost my job. This period allowed me to see a wider opportunity, although it was stressful. I did not pay attention to my health, so I became sick and collapsed at one point. Amid these challenges, my brother's plan for me to pursue a Master's in the UK emerged and I reluctantly embraced it.

I arrived in the United Kingdom for my master's at Sheffield Hallam University to study Public Health during restricted movement. Settling in was not easy, and online classes made it challenging to connect with classmates. I struggled academically, coping with a different teaching style and my health recovery. Challenges persisted, including difficulties with food, weather, and the academic shift from laboratory research background to sociological research and from classroom-based exams to an essay assessment. Writing is not what I enjoy doing, especially academic writing.

Despite these challenges, I recognised the need to improve my writing skills and saw it as a task that needed to be completed. I attended almost all the library webinars and writing dissertation classes. The struggle continued with dissertation extensions and module retakes, but I persevered and made the library my second home. It was tiring and frustrating to see myself still doing what my mates had done and forgotten about. I remember someone asked me if I will be able to finish my dissertation. I was not sure, but I gave a positive response saying yes. My mum was always supporting with her prayers and gave her little assistance to see it progressing. I also, had some of my friends help until the end.

After submission, a heavy burden was lifted off me, but I still worried about the result. Then I had thought to make use of the time I had left with the university. I got involved in extracurricular activities to ease the stress. I volunteered with the student union on beach cleaning and another volunteer role through the union with Sheffield City Council for Basal removal. I signed up as a mentor on the Culture Connect Mentorship programme, worked for the university as a student ambassador and signed up for the Global Citizenship Portfolio. Then I began to enjoy the moments at university. Despite my struggles, surprisingly my results were excellent, reflecting my determination and effort.

I learnt even when the world seems against you and everything is not working for you, believe in yourself and continue to believe. Keep going, keep your hopes high and give it your best. Although, I am not where I want to be, I am on track to my destination as a work in progress. I dedicate this chapter to God Almighty, my mum and my siblings.

# A FAMILIAR SERIES OF EVENTS, A WEALTH OF SPECIFIC LESSONS!

## BY MILLENNIUM IYOBUCHIEBOMIE

I grew up in a household of academics; my mother was an excellent teacher, and my father was a brilliant lecturer and is now a professor. Both have positively impacted many people's lives through their love for education. They poured their hearts into their job and were loved by their colleagues and students. Even after graduating, some students kept in contact with them years later and usually expressed how they benefited from their expertise and interest in them. This environment significantly influenced who I am today - a lover of people and knowledge. I decided to follow in my father's footsteps and pursue a career as a lecturer and researcher. I aim to become a trailblazer in my field, sharing knowledge and positively impacting the lives of my students and everyone I encounter.

Growing up and achieving my career goals has not been easy, and in this piece, I will be focusing on the challenges I faced in my education and career. I always admired my dad's work and how he engaged in activities related to his job. He would talk about giving lectures, supervising students, and conducting research. Still, in my growing mind, I thought about how I could reach a level of proficiency where I could train individuals who would use those skills in different fields and hold various positions of responsibility in society. Although my teachers and peers had different opinions about my intelligence and abilities, that feeling within me was deep-seated. Notwithstanding, through my academic journey, I have pushed and worked hard and have emerged with flying colours; however, not without the support and assistance of well-meaning individuals. This thrilling journey has shaped my character and built my resilience, taking me to where I am today in my career.

I will begin with my undergraduate days to expound on the journey. During my first year of studies, I struggled to transition from secondary to university life, which impacted my grades. However, I was fortunate to have a supportive mentor, Dr. Endurance Uzobo, who believed in me and recognised my potential. With his guidance and the help of my supervisor, Dr. Grace Scent, as well as my hard work, I was able to overcome this obstacle and achieve excellent grades. At the end of my studies, they encouraged me to pursue a career in academia and apply for my master's degree immediately after graduation, which I initiated but did not proceed due to financial constraints and other commitments. At that point, I decided that it was in my best interest not to pursue it, as I lacked the confidence to do so even though, deep within, it was my career goal. However, after nine years, I finally took the step to getting a master's degree.

During my master's programme, I faced several challenges. Imposter syndrome was constantly lurking around, and the long break from academia made it even more difficult. I also struggled with the method of teaching and assessment, which differed from what I was accustomed to. Additionally, the weather conditions were unfavourable and immensely impacted my health. However, I persevered and overcame these difficulties with the help of my ever-supportive family, well-meaning friends, and my awesome husband. I achieved good grades, but not the outcome I envisaged, and this, again, was a setback to my confidence in pursuing a career in academia.

Notwithstanding, my husband encouraged me to consider doing a PhD. However, I was not inclined to do so and decided to look for a job instead. During my job search, I came across the Accomplished Study Programme in Research Excellence (ASPIRE) led by Dr Francis Ifedapo Awolowo, an exceptional individual. The program's principles aligned with my career goals, so I enrolled. The program boosted my confidence in my abilities, taught me practical skills toward building a career in academia and gave me the support I needed through personalised mentorship. This opportunity marked a defining moment in my career, it was the first step in overcoming the imposter syndrome, taking a bold leap into academia, and securing a PhD scholarship.

The journey towards self-actualisation and achieving my career goals taught me valuable lessons. Our choices and connections affect our experiences and success as a student and beyond. Building a sound support system and connecting with the right peers significantly influenced my student experiences. During my undergraduate days, I had good friends who collaborated with me in reading and assessment and supported me through many challenges, especially when I had result-related issues. My master's programme was not any different. Since I had left academia for quite some years, I came this time feeling estranged from the community with no real serious-minded peer support for some time, which significantly impacted my student experience. Still, soon enough, I connected with a few who believed in me, highlighted my academic abilities, and encouraged me to go for it.

A more recent example of support I received was during my time on the ASPIRE programme and in the process of securing a PhD scholarship. One of my cohort members, who later became a dear friend, directed me to available offers and kept me motivated when the imposter syndrome crept in. In addition, the ASPIRE program provided the opportunity to hear from our peers through podcasts and live speeches about their challenges and how they overcame them through perseverance, hard work, and mentorship. Observing individuals who share my experiences and excel in various fields gives me the confidence to pursue my aspirations.

As expressed above, I have encountered various challenges and obstacles in my education and towards attaining my career goals, the most prominent being the imposter syndrome – the feeling of inadequacy and inability to fit into a desired space. However, I have realised that perseverance, resilience, hard work, delayed gratification, and dedication are essential to overcoming different challenges and earning the respect of like-minded peers and seniors within and outside your field of interest willing to provide guidance and support. Some peers who heard of my desire to enter academia felt it was impossible and urged me to take a seemingly "easier" path. Still, the imposter syndrome reduces to its lowest when you have good support from peers and mentors who consistently remind you that you are enough and able to succeed in your field; of note in this regard were my outstanding mentors, Dr. Isaac Danat, Dr. Richard Crisp and Dr Ifeoma N. Onyeka who went above and beyond to give me the motivation I needed and helped me secure a PhD scholarship.

In conclusion, although I struggled with imposter syndrome for a long time, I overcame it by staying focused on my goals, surrounding myself with like-minded peers, being intentional, seizing opportunities to improve myself, and deferring gratification. I owe much of my success to the almighty God Jehovah, who showered me with favour, strength, and fantastic people - my husband, family, well-meaning friends and mentors who believed in, motivated, and supported me. I am eternally grateful for their support. Reflecting on my journey, I realise that if I could go back in time, I would tell my 16-year-old self that self-imposed limitations are unnecessary and a waste of valuable time. Instead, that time should be used productively towards achieving one's goals. These experiences and lessons have informed my writing, with the hope that readers can learn from them. A wise saying summed it nicely: "Do not give up on doing what is fine, for in due time, you will reap if you do not tire out." To my beloved readers, I will say, remain diligent, trust in your abilities and don't give up. If I can overcome self-doubt and continue to thrive, you too can!

# A JOURNEY OF RESILIENCE AND TRIUMPH
## BY OGHENETEGA (CYNTHIA) AWHARITOMA

The theme of 'a journey of resilience and triumph' serves as a narrative thread that weaves through my story having faced adversity, challenges, and setbacks, defying limitations, and emerging stronger and wiser. This theme resonates across cultures, generations, and personal experiences, encapsulating tales of resilience, determination, and triumph over adversity.

I believe my story will encourage black women to never give up regardless of their circumstances especially mothers faced with systemic challenges, societal expectations, and gendered and racial biases.

As a young girl from an average background in Yola, Adamawa state, Nigeria, I had a progressive and seamless education, from graduating with flying colours from high school at age 16, to gaining admission to the university where I got my first degree at age 21. I remember the night before I took my A levels, my parents sat me down, advising me on the need to take my studies seriously with dedication, bearing in mind the prize and making me understand that a good name is better money. Those words kept me going, kept me focused, and made me graduate with flying colours.

## My career in Nigeria

After my first degree, I proceeded immediately to a mandatory 1-year National Youth Service Corps programme in a village called Ikoyi-ile, Ogbomoso, Oyo State, Nigeria where I met my husband.

I got married at 22 years old and got my first professional job working with Marie Stopes International, an international non-governmental organisation in Sokoto, Nigeria as a finance and admin assistant. With commitment, dedication, supportive line managers and colleagues, I was able to rise to a mid-level position in my career.

Being a full-time working mum of 3 kids was never easy as I kept moving up in my career, but I was unable to further my education as I wanted to, looking at the challenges of juggling family, work, and school. I went back to school in 2018 after 8 years for my postgraduate diploma in management as I realised a huge gap in my education and had the nudge to bridge that gap. This was done with so much determination, support systems at my workplace and my family. It was not easy as it took a toll on me, the stress, anxiety and, mental stress, having to keep up with my work deliverables, my school assignments and projects but my parents' advice kept me going remembering what my mum told me that nothing good comes easy and that there's always light at the end of the tunnel and I have to keep my eyes on the prize.

In 2021, a friend encouraged me to look at a master's programme in the UK since I have over 9 years of working experience in international humanitarian and development work. At first, I was scared and wondered if this was going to be possible looking at my family, the finances involved, and the challenges that come with it. Informing and convincing my husband about this step was one of the hurdles I faced as he seemed not to believe in my plan. This weighed me down as I did not get the support I needed, but I kept pushing, making enquiries about deferring my admission for 2022. At this point, my husband noticed I was not backing down and was so determined to make this work regardless of my fears and concerns.

## School in the UK

One of my fears was leaving my kids in Nigeria and not having them around me, I never wanted that. I left Nigeria on 11 September 2022, ensuring I had secured good accommodation for my family before they could join me. Upon resuming my studies in September 2022, I was determined to put in effort for my studies to graduate with a good result, as I had to sacrifice sleeping at night to work on assignments both group and individual tasks. I did this while juggling my children's school runs, my lectures, and going grocery shopping. There were times I cried at night or when having my bath but having my children around me boosted my confidence and inspired me. At this point, I remembered how my mum juggled her master's programme with me and my siblings and how she graduated with a distinction. I drew strength from her story and kept pressing on.

One of the challenges I faced was finance, as I was unable to work because I was alone with my kids while my husband was in Nigeria, although he sent funds for our upkeep it was not sufficient as the exchange rate was on the increase. Although he had to move in with us in 2023.

## Working in the UK

Like other international students with their families in the UK, I faced countless rejections before securing a short-term job in January 2023. I was a workshop assistant with the Association of Science Education (ASE) conference which took place in Sheffield. I did this work while preparing for my project management exams. I continued applying to other recruitment agencies and finally got a job with Tradewind Recruitment as a cleaner, teaching assistant, and school administrator all on a part-time basis (20 hours per week).

While in school, I made sure I improved my essay-writing skills by reading articles on Twitter and other social media platforms. Engaging in these platforms built my confidence regardless of the challenges I faced daily.

## Overcoming mental and emotional challenges:

Amid the mental and emotional challenges, I was able to engage with the wellbeing unit of my school who provided support and made sure I was okay while working on my dissertation. I was also able to help the women around me who were faced with similar challenges by providing a little support, ensuring that they did not succumb to any pressure.

My thanks go to a friend who told me about TG Consulting, a platform where I can share my story to encourage other black women to believe in themselves and rise above any storm life throws at them. Yes, you can achieve anything with the right support system around you. Nothing is impossible.

If I was to offer one piece of advice to my 16-year-old self it would be to accept the process of self-discovery and not be scared to make mistakes. Life is a collection of events, and each one, favourable or negative, contributes to your development. Don't let fear of failure stop you; instead, use it as an opportunity to learn and grow. Your uniqueness is your strength, so embrace it and don't be excessively worried about fitting into preconceived models. Be curious, follow your passions, and remember that external affirmation does not determine your worth. Trust the process, trust in yourself, and remember that every step forward, no matter how tiny, is a win.

# NO EXPIRY DATE ON GRIEF
## BY OLIVIA OLOGBENIA

## A little about me

I was born in Manchester to a Caribbean mother and a Nigerian father so you can imagine how much the importance of education was drilled into me from a young age. My mother was born and grew up in Manchester and studied at Birmingham University, whilst dad came to this country on a scholarship from Oxford University. My dad was always learning, and his aspirations were never limited to any box. Whenever I felt like I couldn't do something, it was my dad that would say "why not? Do the people who can, have two brains?" This draws a picture of how much he made sure to always remind me of my capabilities even when I did not believe in them myself.

## Before university

Like most students I was both excited and nervous for the new chapter of my life that would begin once I started university. I think before we go to university, we all have a preconceived view that this is where your life starts and these are the greatest years of our lives which for most, I think we realised would not be the case. Whether it be due to the stress people have around their assignments or the nervousness of being in a new city away from home for the first time I think mental health at university is something that affects a lot of people.

## During university

I learned more about myself whilst studying as I also had to deal with other things going on in my life outside of university. During my time of study, I lost my dad to cancer. Going through something to this magnitude is definitely something that you never get over. It has affected me in every single way that you can imagine. I remember as a child watching stand up to cancer and seeing that 1 in 4 people get cancer but as they always say you never think it will happen that close to home. Now that number has changed to 1 in 2.

Of course, some days are harder than others and it's still hard for me to think about the fact he is gone forever. When you lose someone, it feels like people expect you to get over it, but as time moves on, you're still stood in the exact same place. For me I felt like life had lost its colour and everything was so bleak. I really felt hopeless and through losing him I've learned that there is really no expiry date on grief, and we all grieve in our own ways.

Losing my dad not only affected me emotionally but it also affected my studies. It gave me a lot of anxiety and stress to meet the deadlines for my assignments and to keep up with everything at university even though I had missed lectures and seminars. Although it was difficult, I knew I had to continue and complete everything to the best of my ability, despite all that I was going through as I still wanted to make myself and my dad proud.

## What I've learnt

The advice that I would give to my 16-year-old self is to be bold and confident. I would tell her that things don't always go the way that you want, but you can't control everything. I would tell her that I am proud of her and to treasure every single moment as one day you will wish you could go back and experience it again, especially all the moments that I had with my dad.

I wanted to share my story as I think parental grief is something other people can relate to, and I hope that through reading this people will also see that they are not alone. For me, speaking with other people who were also going through the same thing was somewhat comforting. It made me feel like people understood exactly how I was feeling and that was something that also helped me deal with my grief. So, I hope I can be that comfort for someone else. I also wanted to share a different side of university that maybe other people haven't considered before.

Mental health will always be a topic that should be talked about more. It's even more important at university as young people leave home to live in a different city by themselves it's easy to feel isolated when you're alone and don't know anyone. I'm blessed to have such an amazing family, but I think about all the people who go to university and don't have a good support system.

My advice to any student who is going onto university is that no matter what you are going through you need to give yourself grace. We're still so young and we're still learning about ourselves so it's okay to make mistakes. I think we are so used to comparing ourselves to those around us who are also the same age or in the same field but when it comes down to it, we are all running our own individual race. Comparison after all is the thief of joy.

Never forget that you are not defined by how many marks you get on your assignment or on an exam. It's a big achievement to go to university and get a degree but also remember that your worth extends far beyond academic success.

Another piece of advice I would give for students is to find something that makes you happy it can be anything e.g. joining a society, finding a hobby outside university and keep finding ways to meet new people. What helped me through everything that I was going through was my faith as a Christian and my love for reading. Reading to me is something that brings me joy and helps me escape too anywhere. I hope someone might read this and see that although things are hard in their life they just have to keep going.

I thank God for every moment that I did have with my dad standing by my side as I was so blessed to have him. He is my inspiration; he is my driving force and the very reason why I will never give up. He is the reason I don't take anything for granted and he is the reason that I know my dreams could never be limited to any box.

I hope that my story can be a testament of resilience and strength. I'm proud of myself that I didn't let my adversities overcome me and that through it all I found a way to carry on and I can't wait until the day I graduate, and I can say that I have made my dad proud.

# REALISATION OF A LOST DREAM
## BY OYENIKE AKINLABI

Just like a twinkling star, I wondered where you are.

When and how I lost you, I did not know.

I realised I had a dream the day I found you.

I found my dream at Sheffield Hallam University (SHU).

ASPIRE gave me her shoulder to lean on.

I am on the path to the fulfilment of my dream.

And I can never underestimate my network's impact in realising my dream.

## The lost dream

I had dreams, just like every aspiring child with vision. I had a mapped-out plan regarding the age I intend to graduate from the University, get married at 25, and have my third child by 35 years of age. Oh, my career aspiration was great. Having the acronym "Dr" in front of my name is one of my dreams. I plan to start my career in the industry and end it in the academic world. Gaining admission into the University was a nightmare for me. Eventually, I opted for a Diploma Course in Accounting after so many years of waiting to be admitted for a degree course. At the time, I felt farther away from attaining my dreams as planned.

Having no knowledge of social science subjects, I found my Accounting Diploma Course exciting and easier than expected. My O'level subjects were purely sciences, as I had wished to be a pharmacist earlier. I decided to graduate with good grades and use my diploma results to gain admission into the University's second year for a full-time degree course in accounting. The most important thing here was that the Diploma Course in Accounting was a revelation of where my passion and interest lie. I am still unsure if I would have loved Pharmacy more. I realised that sometimes our strength does not lie where we think it is, mostly at an earlier stage in life when we make life decisions.

While awaiting the result of my diploma course, I enrolled for the Associate Accounting Technician Course (AAT) of the Institute of Chartered Accountants of Nigeria (ICAN). Enrolment in the ICAN program changed my reading habits tremendously. This was because accounting as a course covers a wider scope, significantly broadening my knowledge and improving my analytical skills. I was preparing for the second stage of the AAT exams when my diploma result was released. I achieved the required grade for a degree programme and became the happiest person on earth. Little did I know I still have oceans to cross on my journey of becoming.

Yes, I gained admission into the University, but a mighty ocean lay ahead of me. I bid my friends goodbye as I carry my luggage to commence a degree course in accounting. I have many aspirations, believing that the sky is my starting point, having undergone ICAN elementary professional training. I could not cross the hurdle that awaited me at the faculty level of the University. After getting screened at the departmental level, the faculty did not screen me. They requested social science O'level subjects, rejecting my science subjects result. These were the same O'levels I used for my diploma course at the same University. The departmental head confirmed that I am qualified for admission. At the time, I was a shadow of myself, and my dreams were becoming shattered.

While preparing for the next stage of my AAT examination, I waited for the issue to be resolved alongside other students affected by the power tussle between the department and the faculty. Days went by, and I resumed at the faculty every blessed morning. Was the morning really blessed? Hell no! The support of my parents, who have an unwavering love for me and my siblings regardless of any weakness, kept me going during this period. What would have happened if I was not surrounded with love?

When the semester's examination was around the corner, and I could not see any limelight, I returned home in shame into the arms of my loving family. To date, I am still trying to figure out what I would have done differently. My faith in God waivered. I renounced him, thinking of why I had to suffer, having waited so long for admission into the University. Today, I boldly say "He is a faithful God whose ways always differ from ours."

## The change agent

It is never too late to start over again. That was the word my father whispered in my ears. I enrolled for GCE and an examination for entry into the first year of the University. I aced the examinations, but I failed the AAT level 2. Eventually, I gained admission into a prestigious university for a degree course in accounting while I continued my ICAN programme concurrently with my degree. I was proud of the young lady I was becoming. I realised that change is a natural part of life, time, generation, and season change. Aiming for a change is desiring growth. With planning and self-awareness, I can achieve my goal.

I aspired to graduate with a First-Class degree from the University. Considering my strengths and weaknesses, I planned to write my ICAN examination during the University season holiday. Following my plans, I graduated from the University with a second-class upper and qualified as a chartered accountant the same year. At this time, I have learned that there is no stagnation in growth, so there is no time when I must maintain the status quo.

## The realised dream

I desire to have a master's degree in accounting or forensic accounting. However, I wished to earn this degree at a western university. I was admitted to South Wales University for the MSc in Forensic Audit and Accounting. However, I had to decline the offer when my application for the Chevening Scholarship was unsuccessful. After three years, I gained admission to the same University for the same course, but funding still needed to be improved. Additionally, I was offered to study MSc Accounting and Finance at Liverpool University with a Commonwealth scholarship of £2,000 and a PGT Vice-Chancellor's International Attainment Scholarship of £2,500 for the reward of excellent academic performance to date, yet I couldn't afford the tuition. An offer for a Master of Administration at New Brunswick University, Canada, was another offer I could not take due to financial constraints.

Against all odds, when I gained admission into Sheffield Hallam University (SHU), I told myself it was time to progress. Funding the master's degree in accounting and finance at Sheffield Hallam University was no easy feat. I aim to finish with an excellent result, and my next step is to return to the industry. Before this time, I had forgotten my dream of having a doctorate. I cannot explain how and when this happened. Perhaps this may be due to funding. Doing my postgraduate in my home country was not an option I had ever considered.

While doing my master's programme, fate connected me with ASPIRE (Accomplished Study Programme in Research Excellence). ASPIRE aims to enable black and black-heritage UK-domiciled students to navigate structural barriers to doctoral study and enhance pathways of opportunity through inclusive targeting. ASPIRE rekindled my passion for the lost dream of bagging a doctorate while funding still poses a problem. I remembered a conversation with one of my mentors on ASPIRE who told me, "If it is what you want, go for it. Do not allow funds to be a barrier to attaining your dream." He added that there may be opportunities tomorrow.

Eventually, I got an offer for one of the ring-fenced doctoral opportunities on ASPIRE. ASPIRE opened the door for a fully funded scholarship. Here comes the opportunity my mentor talked about. The most meaningful experience here was that it is better to act courageously and be willing to face challenges rather than look back with regret.

When I reflect on my journey from childhood to date, the role of people cannot be underestimated. While I lived and grew up under the watch of my lovely parents, a loving woman (I call her mother) in my neighbourhood who doubles as a family friend took it upon herself to teach me how to read when I had difficulty reading. Having mentors on ASPIRE also changed my perspectives. SHU provided access to funding, enabling the achievement of my long-term dream.

Like a twinkling star above the world so high, I found my dream at SHU and am on the path to its fulfilment. After all, I have experienced, I realise it is never too late to begin again. Starting all over may be daunting, but growth requires change.

Thank you, SHU.

Thank you, ASPIRE.

Thank you, my MENTORS.

# LIFE'S CRUCIBLE: SHAPING INFLUENCES ON MY IDENTITY

## BY RASHIDAT KAZEEM

I aim to share my personal journey to offer inspiration and support to individuals navigating transitions, whether in their career, switching job roles, or managing the complexities of combining family duties with study. I want others to understand that these periods can be intensely challenging, but it is crucial to take each day as it comes and stay focused on your goals. While the journey may seem arduous at times, there is always a bright light at the end of the tunnel. I hope my story serves as a testament that challenges can contribute to the narrative of success, just as they did in my own experience.

I have always harboured the aspiration to study abroad, driven by a deep desire to immerse myself in the rich tapestry of knowledge and unlock numerous opportunities that such an experience offers. Despite this lifelong dream, the responsibilities of marriage and raising children compelled me to shift my focus towards nurturing a perfect family life. Balancing household duties while working a 9-5 job as a relationship manager in a bank, I began to believe that my academic aspirations were unattainable.

A pivotal moment occurred during a routine day at the office when I encountered a client, a 55-year-old woman pursuing a master's degree in Canada. As we engaged in conversation, she shared her inspiring journey of finally realising her dreams. That night, her story lingered in my thoughts, sparking a profound contemplation of the possibilities that lay ahead. The idea of pursuing a degree in computing, a field entirely unrelated to my current experience and academic background, seized my imagination. It represented a profound personal interest and an unexplored avenue that I was eager to traverse.

With a resolute determination, I committed to pursuing this newfound aspiration despite the weight of my existing responsibilities and commitments. My first significant step was to embark on an aggressive application process to various schools. Eventually, I received admission to SHU, marking a crucial milestone in my journey. The decision to resign from my current job was met with bewilderment from those around me, as many perceived it as a radical move.

Discussions ensued with my husband and children, and their inquiries were numerous, some of which I, too, grappled with uncertainty. Nevertheless, their support became a cornerstone of my pursuit, and together, we made the decision to embrace this transformative journey. It was a collective leap of faith into the unknown, breaking away from the familiar to embark on a path that held the promise of personal and academic fulfilment.

## Navigating challenges: from student struggles to personal triumphs

In the winter of 2022, I embarked on a journey to Sheffield with my family, unaware of the challenges that awaited. The biting cold welcomed us, an unfamiliar sensation that soon became a constant companion. As the frosty winds swept through, I found myself falling ill, questioning the wisdom of my relocation.

Cultural shock hit me like a tidal wave. Back home, warmth and friendliness were the norm, but here, people seemed to mind their own business, leaving me feeling isolated. Navigating the city's streets and adapting to a new teaching style became daily hurdles.

One evening, after a late class, I found myself lost in the dark. Armed only with a map, I struggled to find my way home. It was a fellow student, a newfound friend, who guided me back. Cold and disheartened, I cried myself to sleep that night, doubting if this move was the right choice.

The challenges were relentless struggling in academics as computing was a field totally new to me, juggling a part-time job, managing childcare, and grappling with the relentless weather and cultural disparities. The weight of it all nearly pushed me to the brink, making me question if returning home was the only way out.

In the midst of my struggles, I reached out to a trusted friend who I will always cherish, pouring out the challenges that seemed insurmountable. She, in turn, suggested a visit to a student advisor, assuring me that things could get better. Skepticism lingered, but I decided to take her counsel, a decision that would alter my course.

As I shared my academic woes with the advisor, he enlightened me about specialised classes designed for students facing similar hurdles. The prospect of additional classes
    meant a more hectic schedule—balancing coursework, a part-time job, and lengthy library sessions. Sleep became a luxury, with nights

spent shuttling between responsibilities. The sacrifices were palpable, especially in terms of family time.

Yet, amid the struggles, my husband emerged as an anchor of unwavering support. His belief in my capabilities surpassed my own, and his encouragement echoed through the trying times. It was a period of challenge, with every moment demanding resilience.

However, from the crucible of adversity, a transformation occurred. These trials became the raw material for personal growth and excellence. Each day brought its share of difficulties, but the journey became a testament to perseverance and the strength that emerges from embracing challenges.

I persisted through the struggles, and as the first term season ended, the results were a testament to my resilience. While not perfect, I had passed all my exams with scores exceeding the average. Simultaneously, my commitment at my part-time job earned me a commendation, and my family had settled into a comfortable routine.

This marked a defining moment—despite shedding tears, discussing my results with my husband, I felt genuine pride. Overcoming the overwhelming challenges built my resilience, halting thoughts of returning home. Making new friends and rediscovering my passion, I embraced the future with newfound determination.

Completing my studies with good grades was a significant achievement, yet the job search comes with its frustrations. Receiving unfortunate rejection emails hasn't deterred my belief in myself and the anticipation of securing a great opportunity soon. Life, though challenging, is a journey taken one step at a time, and I am determined to make the most of it.

## Themes of resilience and growth: evoking emotions in my story

Embarking on this transformative journey felt like navigating a labyrinth of challenges, from the disorienting cultural shocks to the biting cold that tested the limits of my resolve. There were moments when the idea of turning back loomed large, and despair threatened to cast a shadow over my aspirations. However, this narrative is more than a mere chronicle of struggles; it's a tale of resilience, a journey that unfolded amidst the cold, weaving threads of warmth, and emerging stronger from the crucible of adversity.

As I journeyed through the lows of despair to the highs of personal triumphs, each chapter of this story became infused with emotions, portraying the transformative power inherent in challenges. Every obstacle transformed into a steppingstone towards growth, whether it was the struggles in academics, the delicate balancing act of work and childcare, or the adaptation to an entirely new environment. These challenges became threads intricately woven into the fabric of resilience.

Sharing my story as an international student is an attempt to connect with individuals globally who might be facing similar challenges. Through the exploration of foreign academics, cultural nuances, and the pangs of homesickness, I discovered the profound transformative power that resilience holds. My earnest intent is to extend a hand of encouragement to fellow students, urging them to persevere through challenges and face each day with an unwavering belief in the attainability of their dreams.

This narrative serves as a guiding light for those studying abroad, underlining the significance of self-discovery and growth. Taking life one day at a time enables students to overcome overwhelming hurdles while maintaining a steadfast focus on their ultimate goals. I implore readers to recognise that dreams are enduring beacons, unextinguishable by any challenge, serving as guiding lights through life's storms.

I hope that readers, irrespective of their national or cultural background, find inspiration in my chapter. I encourage them to pursue their dreams with unwavering determination, regardless of distractions or obstacles. Each dream, I believe, holds inherent worth, contributing to the fulfilment of life's journey. Through shared experiences, I aspire to impart the wisdom that success is not devoid of challenges but is, in fact, shaped by the resilience to conquer them. May this story stand as a testament to the indomitable spirit within each person, urging them to reach for the stars and turn their dreams into tangible realities.

In conclusion, my story evolves into a celebration of victories against the odds. It transcends the mere conquest of academic hurdles or professional excellence; it's about finding stability at home amidst chaos. By sharing this transformative journey, my intent is to ignite inspiration among those confronting challenges, illustrating that resilience and growth can flourish even in the darkest corners. The resounding message is one of encouragement — a call for others to persist, embrace challenges, and believe in their innate ability to triumph over adversity, mirroring the triumphs within my own story. May this narrative serve as a beacon of hope, echoing the indomitable human spirit's capacity to overcome and flourish.

# CHASING THE DREAM
## BY SOPEFOLUWA OLUYIDE

My story will inspire everyone, especially international students with different cultural backgrounds, that nothing can stop anyone, not even the colour of one's skin or one's cultural background, if one follows the rules of success, such as hard work, determination to succeed and believing in oneself even in the face of adversities. Always remember, "it costs nothing to believe in yourself, but it will cost you everything if you don't" – Joel Brown.

## The journey from Africa to Europe

Chasing one's dreams sometimes involves leaving one's comfort zone to embark on a journey one isn't sure of. The validity of the dreams and the self-assurance that the dream will come true drives and keeps one going despite the bleak weather and blurred vision.

I took a leap of faith in 2021 by leaving my parents, with whom I am so connected, and my job to study for a master's programme in the United Kingdom. My choice of university to study was borne out of my interest in the course modules compared to other institutions where I got admission and the dearth of institutions offering the course in my home country. I had fears and reservations about going to another country to study, but I decided that I would make myself and my family proud as I had always done.

## My ordeal as a student

Coming to the United Kingdom for my Masters's programme wasn't a bed of roses like I had envisaged. The first 17 days of my landing in the country were spent in a hotel as we needed a place for the 10-day quarantine due to COVID-19 restrictions rules for foreigners. Afterward, securing accommodation as a family of 3 became a nightmare. I remember having sleepless nights and weeping profusely some nights as I was eager to settle down and start classes at the right time but couldn't meet the 6-month pay slip requirement of many landlords contacted as we had just come in and were not employed yet.

My family eventually secured a short-term apartment, which turned out to be dubious. Receiving the news of invaders in my apartment on one of the days I was studying in the library left me devastated, but I saw it as a distraction to my dream. However, I knew "being challenged in life is inevitable, but succumbing to defeat was my choice." – Roger Crawford. Therefore, I chose not to let that beat me down. Adapting to western culture also took me a while as a perfectionist. It wasn't easy for me to shift and change in bits as I ought to because I longed for a drastic shift, which is apparently against the nature of change.

I heard in one of the welcome sessions I had in my first week of resumption that effective communication is one of the factors that enables success. Although the major *lingua franca* in Nigeria is English, I worried that non-Africans wouldn't understand my accents. This struggle wasn't from my end alone; I also had difficulties understanding other non-African accents. I remember my first class with a white lecturer; even though I prepared for the class by reading the topic to be covered, I found it hard to pick just a sentence throughout the 120 minutes of his teaching. Other white students in class laughed many times and responded to his questions, which assured me he was communicating, but I couldn't pick up his words. I wept this very day as I was eager to understand him; this made me strategically increase my preparations before going to his class and securing my seat right in front of him, even if it would make me get to class an hour before class to secure the space as I wasn't ready to give in to self-defeat.

At the start of my course, I struggled with imposter syndrome, which made me feel less of myself. I felt inadequate at some point, especially when I realised that education in the UK was very different from what I was already used to. The saying that "the top is meant for a particular set of people" almost got into me, and I almost succumbed to it until I embraced the popular saying of A.A Miine that "I am braver than I believe, stronger than I seem, and smarter than I think." I improved as each day passed because I was intentional that I would give it all it takes to succeed.

Being a person of many shades is often referred to as one of the strengths of a woman, but it can be draining when she adds being a student to it. Taking up the responsibility of being a wife, a mother, and a student in a country where you feel lonely was not an easy task, but like other hurdles, I intentionally decided to cross it and beat it. I can't imagine how I survived when my toddler-turned-guidance angel would remain next to me with her book and pen in her tiny hands, trying to write out as many words as I typed on my computer even if I stayed awake all through the night. Even at the point of giving up, as the one-year programme was highly rigorous, I reassured myself that I could do it no matter what came my way. Yes! I believed I could do it!

## My success factors

Many factors contributed to my success, but to mention a few. A word that could describe my drive for success is tenacity. I do not give up and never let go, no matter what. I often felt down because I didn't get my expected marks and felt like letting go, but I see failure as a reason to try harder and put more strength into getting trophies. Hard work and determination paved many ways for me, and my curiosity with strong desire to learn made me stand out. I accepted that "success does not come to us, but we go to it" – Mawa Collins, and it's true that "A dream doesn't make a reality through magic, but it takes sweat, determination, and hard work."

My upbringing helped me on this journey; I had always been inspired by my parents, and I believe so much in their values. I remember growing up; my father would always tell me to put my best in everything and do it well so I don't regret not doing something I should have done. I watched him closely as I grew, and I discovered that the secret to his wealth of knowledge and excellence as an academic is his passion for knowledge and ability to always put his best foot forward. These imbibed values make me give my best to whatever I do. No wonder a colleague I met in one of my casual jobs in the early months of my study asked why I was working like a new staff placed on probation. I smiled in my mind as I knew he felt I was putting too much effort into a shift I might not be lucky to get the following day.

I was lucky to join the ASPIRE (Accomplished Study Programme in Research Excellence) programme at the start of my second trimester. The programme addresses the continuing inequalities that create barriers for BAME students. A lot of organized workshops and seminars on ASPIRE enhanced my perspectives on success and helped boost the confidence I have in myself that nothing should stop me from achieving the best. What stood out was when I was assigned a female mentor of my colour who has successfully navigated the UK educational system. This reassured me of my dreams and motivated me. In addition, having BAME lecturers in my department was the icing on the cake for me. I had people of my colour to relay my fears to, with the mindset that they would understand my plight.

Reaching out for help also contributed to my success. The triangle support: the academic adviser, employability adviser, and student support adviser provided by the institution were helpful as they all served their purposes at some point in my studies. I also took advantage of the Skill Centre support from the library. The workshops and seminars helped shape my academic and critical writing and gave me insights to improve my studies. The department lecturers also gave their best, and I was not hesitant to seek clarification when needed, as they were willing and eager to provide help.

Furthermore, receiving constructive feedback from tutors helped me improve my performance and motivated me. I remember the feedback I got from my white lecturer, whose accent I didn't understand in my first class. He wrote, "…147 footnotes-excellent, a very impressive answer and one to be proud of, very well done Sopefoluwa." I read this comment over 100 times during my studies, as I wouldn't have imagined a white lecturer calling me by name and giving me such accolades. This singular feedback encouraged me to put more effort into my studies and brought me more accolades. Surely, "self-belief and hard work will always earn one success"- Virat Kohli.

Lastly, the most appealing driver of my success was the support I got from my family. I am so blessed with wonderful people who are interested in my success. My parents have been my strong pillar since the inception of my life, and they were so supportive throughout my programme. My siblings were very present, and my husband gave his all to ensure I fulfil my dream. Literally, I was only a representative of these people as they were my cheerleaders.

Success is sweet, so they say. I graduated from the department with distinctions in all the modules and as the best graduating student with an in-depth understanding of the course. There was a dramatic transformation in my attitude to work as I learned that there are rewards for hard work. I also acquired more personal and professional skills, and the one-year journey reassured me of my career path as I could confirm where my interest and career fulfilment lie.

For every dream, there are challenges and obstacles. However, persistence and resilience make the dream come true. Using the right approach, such as hard work, seeking help, when necessary, mentorship, and self-belief, makes no mountain insurmountable. Always remember, "It costs you nothing to believe in yourself, but it will cost you everything if you don't" – Joel Brown. Nothing is impossible to achieve; the word itself says I'm POSSIBLE!

# ASPECT OF LIFE
## BY TIMILEHIN MOSES

From the earliest days of my primary education, a steadfast commitment to learning became the cornerstone of my identity. Reflecting upon those formative years, I recall a relentless dedication to my studies, evident in the unwavering presence of my name on the attendance register from the commencement to the culmination of each term. Even when health concerns prompted my class teacher to escort me home, the very next day I would find myself triumphantly returning to the school compound, leaving teachers puzzled at my resilience in overcoming health challenges.

My commitment to education was not only a personal endeavor but a testament to a broader philosophy that learning was not just a duty but a calling. The profound belief in the transformative power of education shaped my approach to life from an early age. It was an unspoken pact with myself to embrace every opportunity for intellectual growth and to overcome any obstacle that threatened to hinder my educational journey.

During these foundational years, a pivotal moment arose when someone questioned my audacious aspiration to become an academic. I distinctly remember, as little as I was back then, he assumed it was beyond my reach due to my financial background and my family's social status in society at that time because I grew up in a community where your parents were either teachers or lecturers in a higher institution to become academia. The skepticism wasn't rooted in my abilities or ambitions but rather in the prevailing socio-economic norms of that community back then. The assumption was that a career in academia was exclusively reserved for those with a certain financial background and societal status, typically those whose parents were educators in higher institutions.

This encounter became a catalyst for my determination to challenge such preconceptions. It fueled a fire within me to defy the limiting expectations associated with one's origins and family background. I embraced the conviction that academic pursuits were not exclusive domains, but open pathways for anyone with the passion and commitment to traverse them.

As the years unfolded, this foundational commitment to education remained steadfast. It became the driving force that propelled me through primary and secondary school, laying the groundwork for my journey toward academia. The lessons learned during those early years transcend the confines of textbooks; they encapsulate the resilience, determination, and belief in the universality of educational aspirations. Today, I stand as a testament to the idea that one's origins need not dictate the trajectory of their educational pursuits and that, indeed, anyone can carve a path in academia with unwavering dedication and resilience.

## Challenges and moments that shaped my resilience

Embarking on my academic journey, I encountered financial hardships that would prove to be formidable tests of my resilience. The pivotal moment arrived when I realized that to secure my education and navigate the crucial West African Examinations Council (WAEC), I needed to take matters into my own hands.

I was undeterred by the challenges and rather seized an entrepreneurial opportunity. After school hours, I dedicated my time to hawking freshly boiled groundnuts at the bustling motor park. The aroma of the nuts served as both a savory snack for travelers and a means to finance my education. Each sale brought me a step closer to my goal, and I carefully set aside profits to cover the expenses of extra lessons, which was a strategic investment aimed at ensuring success in the looming WAEC exam.

Post-secondary school, pursuing education continued to be intertwined with the demands of financial responsibility. As a testament to my unwavering determination, I engaged in a variety of employment roles. Serving as a receptionist, I honed my organizational and interpersonal skills. Embracing casual labor, I undertook physical challenges with vigor, knowing that each task completed brought me nearer to my educational aspirations.

The era of audio cassettes found me working within a recording studio, where I immersed myself in the intricate world of audio production. Simultaneously, I took on the role of a video cameraman, maneuvering the equipment to capture moments on tape. These diverse roles were not only means of financial sustenance but deliberate steps in a carefully charted plan to accumulate funds for the pursuit of my academic career.

These challenges, diverse and demanding, became the crucible in which my resilience was forged. Each day of hard work, every extra lesson funded, and each labor-intensive task undertaken contributed to a profound appreciation for the value of education and the sacrifices necessary to attain it.

As I reflect on those formative experiences, I carry forward not just a transcript of academic achievements, but a rich tapestry woven with the threads of dedication, entrepreneurial spirit, and an enduring commitment to the transformative power of education. These challenges have shaped my resilience, instilling in me a profound belief in the immense value that education brings to the individual and society at large.

A profound turning point within my academic odyssey unfolded during my MSc program at Sheffield Hallam University, a period marked not only by academic rigor but also by an invaluable opportunity that reshaped the trajectory of my aspirations.

During what proved to be a challenging space to navigate, a beacon of clarity emerged with the advent of the ASPIRE (Accomplished Study Programme in Research Excellence) program. Spearheaded jointly by Sheffield Hallam University and Manchester Metropolitan University, this initiative became the catalyst for a transformative experience. Despite the inherent difficulties of the academic landscape, my participation in the inaugural edition of the ASPIRE program proved to be a pivotal moment that etched indelible marks on my academic journey.

The ASPIRE programme, in its maiden edition, functioned as more than a mere academic exercise; it was a compass, demystifying the intricate journey toward a Ph.D. and a career path. Its impact transcended the theoretical and offered tangible insights into the world of academia and career advancement. This experience was not solely an illumination of possibilities; it was the rekindling of a fervent dream for me to become an academic force contributing to the collective knowledge of my chosen field.

Navigating the program was akin to unlocking a treasure trove of knowledge, with each session unveiling the nuances of academic progression and shedding light on the pathway to a Ph.D. The program provided not just theoretical insights but practical wisdom, offering a roadmap to navigate the complexities of the academic system.

The clarity gained through the ASPIRE program was not ephemeral; it resonated profoundly in my academic pursuits. Armed with newfound knowledge and fortified aspirations, I set forth on a journey that would culminate in a significant milestone: a fully funded Ph.D. opportunity with Sheffield Hallam University. The lessons imbibed during the ASPIRE program became more than stepping stones; they were the foundation upon which I built the next chapter of my academic voyage.

As I prepare to commence my Ph.D. in early February 2024, I reflect on the significance of that defining moment, the ASPIRE program, an experience that not only demystified the pursuit of a Ph.D. but also reignited the flames of my academic dreams, setting me on a trajectory toward meaningful contributions to my field. The impact of that moment continues to reverberate, shaping not only my academic journey but the very essence of who I am becoming in the world of academia.

One of the most formidable hurdles in my academic journey materialized in the form of a substantial financial barrier impeding my pursuit of a Ph.D. as an international student. The expanse of the tuition fees, even during my MSc program, cast a looming shadow over my aspirations, creating a formidable obstacle that seemed insurmountable. The financial burden, coupled with the prevailing economic challenges, posed a critical test to my determination to advance in academia.

Adding to the complexity of this financial challenge was the revelation of discriminatory practices within certain scholarship opportunities. It was disheartening to discover that some scholarships were exclusively earmarked for individuals of specific nationalities. This discovery underscored the systemic challenges frequently faced by international students, injecting an additional layer of difficulty into the already complex landscape of academic pursuit.

However, it is with immense gratitude and a sense of triumph that I can assert that these challenges - once formidable barriers - now reside in the realm of the past. Through tenacity, perseverance and a commitment to my academic goals, I have successfully secured a fully funded Ph.D. opportunity. This milestone not only symbolizes personal triumph but stands as a testament to the resilience required to navigate the intricate financial and discriminatory challenges that often accompany the pursuit of advanced education as an international scholar.

## Navigating student challenges and personal experiences

Balancing the demands of being a student while dealing with personal challenges was a delicate dance. Hawking at the motor park, working as a casual laborer and studio staff to finance my education during high school taught me valuable time management and perseverance skills. Despite facing adversity, I continued to save and invest in my academic career, reaching the MSc level.

My personal experiences, including financial struggles and discrimination, have significantly impacted my academic journey. These challenges fueled my determination to excel and contribute meaningfully to academia. They also deepened my understanding of the barriers faced by students from diverse backgrounds and motivated me to advocate for inclusivity in education.

Amidst the hurdles and challenges I faced, there were notable instances of relationships with fellow students who, like me, harbored similar aspirations and confronted shared struggles. These connections emerged as pivotal elements in shaping my overall student experience, offering a nexus of support, encouragement, and a profound sense of belonging. Collaborative endeavors with these like-minded peers not only fortified my determination but also became instrumental in surmounting obstacles, propelling me forward on the path toward my academic aspirations.

In conclusion, my journey reflects a commitment to education, resilience in the face of challenges, and a passion for academia. Each experience has contributed to shaping my identity and strengthening my resolve to break barriers in pursuit of knowledge and a career in academia.

I share this story not to boast but to inspire. It's never too late, you have the power to achieve your dream. The journey may be tough, but the destination is worth it. Don't give up on your aspirations. Embrace challenges as opportunities to grow and let your passion drive you toward your goals. Remember, with determination and hard work, you can overcome any obstacle and create the future you desire.

# MY JOURNEY TOWARDS MY DREAM
## BY VEENGUS TALPUR

I came to the United Kingdom in January 2013. I was 23 years old and had a baby boy 2-3 months old. Before I had a chance to go to university in Pakistan, I got married and went to college instead where I studied a bachelor's in commerce (B.com) for two years. I always dreamed of making my career, so when I came to the UK, I kept dreaming the same. At first, I thought, I should choose to study education to become a teacher because my mum is a teacher and she has always been my inspiration. The second benefit of becoming a teacher was to have holidays with my children. Well, going to a college or university in the UK was not easy for me because I came from another country, and I had no professional degree or work experience to get into things easily. I attended open days at Sheffield Hallam University and found out that I had to do a GCSE in English and Maths to get admission to the university. When I went to get admission to the GCSEs, I found that I had to do functional skills courses to complete my GCSEs. Well, I had no choice but to do what I had been told to do.

Finally, in 2016, I got admission in functional skills (English and

Maths). I had two children by this time, aged about 3 and 4. I took on all the responsibilities myself, towards everything such as; groceries, household chores, cooking, picking up and dropping off my children from nursery etc. as every single mother or woman does for their family. I was not driving at that time, and it was very difficult to handle everything, especially during winter when I had to take a bus to go to the college and pick up or drop my children off at nursery. Finally, I completed my functional skills courses in 2017 and then I thought I should get admitted to the teaching assistant level 2 course until I do my GCSEs. I am thankful that I did, because when I finished the teaching assistant course I had to return to my country for a year for personal reasons and I did a teaching job over there - but I did not enjoy it. I found it difficult as it was not my cup of tea. When I came back to the UK, I decided to do an AAT level 2 to see if I would enjoy accounting as I was very good at Maths in school and B.com. From 2018 to 2019, I did AAT level 2 Accounting. I enjoyed it and passed with a distinction. In the meantime, I also did GCSE English, but I could not get the minimum required grade due to the pandemic - grades were given based on class work, and I was not paying much attention because I thought I would do better in exams. Unfortunately, the exams did not happen, and I was worried that if my university admission were conditional based on GCSE English that would mean I would not get the admission. I was disheartened and thinking about what I'd do now. How do I make my career? Will I have nothing? Will I have no professional life?

One day I received an email from the university that I had been admitted to the Accounting and Finance course. It took me a few years to get into the university, but I was glad it happened at last. Finally, I started my university journey in 2020, during a difficult time when the COVID-19 pandemic was at its peak. Studying alone without any interaction was quite challenging. I had always been praised by my tutors for doing so well and for being one of their best students. Hearing all that positivity always encouraged me to do more and more well. On one hand, having online classes were better for me being a mum as I had a good chance to spend time with kids rather than travelling to the university. On the other hand, it was particularly difficult to complete group assessments, as I had never met my classmates. I tried to help my group mates and encouraged them to participate in the group work. Despite the challenges, I managed to pass the first year with flying colours and was among the top 10 students in the Financial Accounting module. I cannot forget that it's all because of my children. They were only 6 and 7 years old, but they had been my pillars of support throughout the tough times such as deadlines, exams, and personal struggles. I am extremely proud of them.

During my second year, in the APS module, I was required to do 120 hours of work to gain soft skills. I applied to many part-time jobs, particularly ones related to my degree, as this would benefit me in future. I got rejections from many places but one day I got two job offers. I was undecided about which one to pick however, I made sensible choices based on pros and cons. I went beyond what was required of me by completing more tasks than necessary and by helping others. My efforts were recognised as I was nominated for the Student

Inspirational Award in two categories. I was even shortlisted for one of them, which was a complete surprise for me. Being nominated for the award was also a big shock for me as I never imagined that somebody could recognise my efforts. This was another moment when I was on top of the moon. I rang my parents and told them that I had been nominated for this and two hours later, I received another email from the university that I had been shortlisted. I can't explain how I was feeling at that moment. I passed my second year with the first classification. Everything was going so well.

Then there was a time to look for a placement and I applied to many places and got many assessments and interview calls. It was a difficult time because it was also time for exams and assignment deadlines. I was packing up for one thing and preparing for another. I interviewed for Cranswick plc and got an offer after a few weeks. Then I stopped preparing for other interviews and assessments, I received a few calls for interviews after the Cranswick offer but I did not bother to attend any more. I did my finance placement at Cranswick plc and now work as a placement representative at university. I am committed to helping other students find their placements. Additionally, I am a Course Representative, representing my peers on the Level 6 course.

Now I am at level 6, studying full-time at the university and working three days a week. It is a challenging time for me, but I never give up and always face challenges and difficult situations. I have also faced many personal difficulties during these years, but I always had a hope that one day everything would be fine. I have learnt one thing; be positive all the time. It's okay if things go in different directions. Since I started university and achieved first classification in previous years, I always aimed to achieve first, but having a difficult time in my final year I am just thinking of getting a pass and it's okay if I get a 2:1 classification. I am still proud of myself for achieving a lot and being recognised by my peers and tutors. My tutors have always praised my hardworking nature and my ability to face challenges. I am grateful to my parents who always pray for me, and my children who understand my situation despite their young age. I also want to share with readers that I have achieved Bronze and Silver Hallam Awards in previous years by taking extra responsibilities, experiences, and facing challenges. This year I am working towards gaining the Gold Hallam Award, which would be a highly achievable recognition of mine on my graduation. After graduation, I will sit for the ACCA exams and step by step will make my career and this journey will continue until I retire or get too old to do anything.

I share my story because I believe many individuals attempt to pursue multiple endeavours, but they may feel overwhelmed with the thought of managing everything and perceive themselves as lagging behind others. I hope my story inspires such individuals to take advantage of the opportunities they come across. I hope that you, the reader, can learn that no matter how difficult the journey towards a dream may be, once it is achieved, all the hardships and struggles faced during the journey are forgotten. The challenges that come with the dream may not be easy, but with passion and perseverance, success will eventually be achieved.

# MY JOURNEY OF 3000 MILES
## BY ZAINAB ATA

Reflecting on my journey, it's clear that the vision my five-year-old self had of the future was far from the reality I find myself in today. Hailing from Kano state, Nigeria, I once pictured myself cruising in a car, owning an apartment, and casually driving to my parent's house on weekends by the age of 23 – a dream that seemed distant. Surprisingly, it's not entirely out of reach; while I may not have checked all those boxes, I embraced full independence at 21 - a goal I had always wanted.

My career path has been a series of shifts sparked by an early desire to be a professor. I vividly recall a photo my mom took of me when I was six, wearing her reading glasses while immersed in Enid Blyton. The dream morphed over the years, leading me to aspirations of becoming a doctor, forensic scientist, computer whiz and, finally, an Environmental Scientist.

The early years are a bit of a blur, with a childhood spent eagerly anticipating adulthood in a loving family surrounded by incredible siblings. In secondary school, I found myself in an all-girls school in Lagos forming unbreakable bonds with some of the best girlfriend's life could offer. My friendship group was quiet, although our set earned the title of "the worst the principal had seen" – a badge of honour, no doubt. The beauty of an all-girls school? Having each other's backs then and now, a bond unbroken by time.

Recalling my experience taking the WAEC (the equivalent of A-levels), I found myself in the dark about which university awaited me. However, I held firm to the belief that good grades would pave the way, making the choice of a university a secondary concern. The nights of staying up all night and revising past examination papers whilst I listened to my reading playlist were fun. The extra lessons and hangout with friends after exams made it pass swiftly. Soon, the results were out and I passed, I had just graduated from secondary school. Now it was the waiting time. I had about three universities I had applied to and I was just waiting for an offer.

The excitement peaked when my mom shared the news that I would be attending a foundation school, potentially opening doors for admission abroad. The transition proved challenging as I switched to a mixed school, suddenly finding myself one of only two girls in my pathway. Amid the expected hurdles of fights, exams and missed classes, the overall experience was enchanting. This period introduced me to some of my closest friends, who remain actively involved in my life to this day.

And there's my childhood friends – the companions on this journey. They weren't just friends; they were co-pilots navigating the bumps and challenges. Journeys can be long and hard, but it's the people you share them with that make the ride worthwhile. As I reflect on where I am now, I realize it's not just about the dreams of a five-year-old; it's about the journey that turned those dreams into a captivating story.

## A pebble in my shoe

Going to a new university was bittersweet. Once again I had to leave a place I had grown to love for a completely new city. I found it frustrating as I felt I was going to be the 'new girl' in class and from movies we have watched it is not always a lovely experience. At times like this, I am grateful that movies aren't reality. Was it hard to form a friendship group when everyone knew each other? Yes, but I guess it is easier when you are studying a course that feels niche. I am introverted, so it did take a while for me to build a connection with my course mates.

After finding my feet and being involved in societies, I felt life settled, but here comes the pandemic. I guess like most people I was not worried about being on lockdown - it felt like paradise on earth for introverted me. Two weeks into lockdown I guess my mental health declined all I wanted to do was lay in bed. My flatmate had gone home and I could not see my family or friends. There were days when I realised I had not said a word. I had to sing to ensure my voice was not gone. That's when I started karaoke every week, just me in my room with a deodorant bottle singing my heart out. Looking back, I never understood how I made it out of lockdown without having a full breakdown, but then again, I don't think anyone made it out the same.

When we were finally let out of lockdown at least here in the UK, I slowly found the courage to try and build friendships when my final year started. I took an active role in the student union and tried out new things. It was in 2021 I felt a light a glimmer of hope, I had been elected to a full-time student union office and that's when I decided to explore the opportunities I had in my hands.

## New beginnings

It was a turning point, full of optimism and uncertainty when I finished my year-long sabbatical. A wave of fear swept through me as I stood at this crossroads, staring into the unknown future. My spirits were down because of my unwavering quest to find out what was ahead. Somewhat brightly, nevertheless, I managed to land a graduate internship in funding at Sheffield Hallam University despite job rejections.

Stepping into this new professional chapter, I was a bit anxious as I had never worked in such a formal professional setting. The initial week in my graduate role was marked by intense pressure as a perfectionist. I really didn't want to make mistakes and I was eager to leave a lasting impression on both colleagues and managers.

But, within a few weeks, I felt a deep sense of security in the encouraging and kind environment of my job. The professional landscape became a supportive place where I could explore my work with confidence and enthusiasm because of the camaraderie I shared with my colleagues.

My everyday routine was made cosier by the relationships I made throughout my internship, which also improved my work experience. We developed a beloved ritual of having weekly one-hour catch-ups with other graduate interns, which gave us an opportunity to catch up with each other. We had to deal with the constant worry of our visas expiring because we were international students, but we handled those conversations well, always returning to the good things about our experience.

After three months, I no longer felt like just an 'intern' and was managing several projects and contributing to the team as a valued member. Concurrently, the month of my graduation approached, marking the pinnacle of my diligence and hard work. The idea of spending time with my family again after a long time excited me more than anything else.

On the gloomy, chilly day of my graduation, I took comfort in getting up early to get ready for the ceremony. The love and joy I experienced with the people closest to my heart gave off a warmth that wasn't caused by the weather.

After the festivities, things slowed down and I tried to find time for hobbies and social gatherings with friends. One notable accomplishment from one of my projects was our team's victory at a Greentech startup event. My life seemed to come together when I was offered a permanent position at Sheffield Hallam University.

Reflecting on this transformative journey, I once believed that the destination outweighed the journey. However, in hindsight, I've come to cherish every path of the experience—the tears, laughter, and the wonderful friendships formed. As I eagerly anticipate new adventures, I realise that the journey itself is a world of emotions and connections that I hold dear. I felt it was essential to share my story as an 18-year-old who took a plane and travelled away from the comforts of home to pursue education in the UK to inspire people and leave a legacy that I will always treasure. My goal is to always be learning and growing, always looking for new adventures that will allow me to be who I truly am. In addition to being committed to my development, I also try to recognise and be proud of the events and successes that have shaped my path.

If I was to offer my 16-year-old self any advice, I'd say: Do not forget to dream big! The world is so vast and there is so much to explore. Seize the opportunity to forge new connections, embrace failure as a stepping stone to learning and above all, remember to live amidst life's chaos.

# ABOUT TG CONSULTING

TG Consulting is an independent education consultancy, specialising in employability, student engagement and social mobility.

Our ethos is to **connect, collaborate** and **create**. Breaking down barriers for students, creating opportunities and building confidence. Daily we engage with students like those whose stories are featured in this book.

**Our bespoke services include:**
Graduate and student employability
Student training and development
Staff training and development
Student Engagement
Embedding employability frameworks and modelling
Graduate outcomes strategy
Careers & Employability strategy
Social Mobility
Racial Equity
Employer engagement alignment

We understand the higher education and student environment well and can provide useful insights into the higher education space including the student journey and recent trends. This will align your campaigns and products, so you have a clear proposition, targeted solution and campaigns.

We offer a range of services from short-term or strategic support to aligning serviced and team structures, so whatever your challenge, drop us a line and we will connect, collaborate, and create.

info@tgconsultingltd.co.uk

www.tgconsultingltd.co.uk

Find us on Instagram and LinkedIn.

# UNIVERSITY RESOURCES AND INFORMATION

While you're at Sheffield Hallam, you'll always have three dedicated advisers to look out for you.

A student **support adviser** to help when outside problems affect your studies.

An **academic adviser** to support your learning journey.

An **employability adviser** to help you choose and build the right career.

Need something else? Please speak to one of our specialist support teams to find the help you need.

## Hallam Help

The Hallam Help Service is here to provide you with high quality support, wherever you need it. In person at Hallam Help Points, via email, phone, Twitter and MyHallam. For more information on Hallam Help visit **https://www.shu.ac.uk/myhallam/help-and-support**

## Multifaith Chaplaincy

The Multifaith Chaplaincy Team consists of representatives and advisers from a wide range of faiths and belief systems. It exists to serve the spiritual and religious needs of everyone studying, working, or associated with the university community of Sheffield Hallam and to promote mutual understanding and respect amongst people of different religious faiths and none, and across all cultures.

## Disabled student support

Disabled Student Support helps over 4,000 students each year who have a variety of conditions. Our disability specialists can answer all types of disability enquiries, assess support needs, and provide support packages.

## Careers and employability

The Careers and Employability Service is here to support you throughout your time at university and beyond with lifelong career advice, in-person and online.

## Student wellbeing

Student wellbeing provides information and advice to support your psychological wellbeing in order for you to manage your studies and make the most of university life.

For more information and to access the Sheffield Hallam University support services visit **https://www.shu.ac.uk/study-here/student-life/support/student-support**.

# HELPFUL ORGANISATIONS

This book is full of inspirational stories to celebrate the strength of these individuals who have overcome adversity and barriers in their lifetime. The content of this book is not intended to be a substitute for professional advice or treatment. Always seek the advice of a mental health professional or other qualified health practitioner.

## Useful resources

**Student Minds**

www.studentminds.org.uk

**Childline**

*If you are under 19 you can call, email or chat online about any problems you have.

www.childline.org.uk/-getsupport/1-2-1-counsellor-chat/

www.childline.org.uk/get-support/contacting-childline/#BSL-counselling - if you need a British Sign Language interpreter.

www.childline.org.uk/get-support/message-boards/ - message boards to talk to other young people in similar situations.

Phone helpline Opening times:

9am - midnight, 365 days a year, 0800 11 11

**PAPYRUS**

Confidential support for under-35s at risk of suicide and others who are concerned about them. Open daily from 9am–midnight.

07860 039967 (text)

pat@papyrus-uk.org

papyrus-uk.org

## OCD Youth

Youth Support for young people with obsessive-compulsive disorder (OCD).

ocdyouth.org

## NHS

NHS app with confidential health advice and support for 16–25-year-olds.

nhsgo.uk

## SANE

Charity that offers emotional support and information to anyone affected by mental health through their out of hours support line.

www.sane.org.uk

## The Mix

13–25-year-olds can receive advice on any problem including discrimination, drugs and money.

Helpline:  0808 808 4994

www.themix.org.uk

## Victim Support

If you've been a victim of any crime or have been affected by a crime committed against someone you know, victim support can help you

find the strength to deal with what you've been through. Services are free and available to everyone, whether or not the crime has been reported and regardless of when it happened.
Support line: 0808 1689 111.

**Stop Hate UK**
A confidential 24-hour support service for young people under 18 experiencing or witnessing a Hate Crime.
www.stophateuk.org/call-hate-out/

**Boloh**
Supports Black, Asian or Minority Ethnic children (11+), young people and parents and carers who have been affected by COVID-19. You can call to talk through any worry or problem. You can speak to someone in English, Gujarati, Urdu, Bengali, French, Spanish, Arabic, Punjabi, Mirpuri, Pothwari, Hinko, Hindi and Sundhi. Interpreters are available for other languages.
 Opening times:10am - 8pm, Monday - Friday; 10am - 3pm on Saturdays and Sundays.
0800 151 2605
Webchat Service: www.helpline.barnardos.org.uk/contact-boloh

**Mencap**
Information and advice for people with a learning disability, their families and carers. Services include an online community.
0808 808 1111
mencap.org.uk

**Scope helpline**

Equality for disabled people

www.scope.org.uk/helpline/

0808 800 3333 and online support


**Diabetes UK Helpline**

0345 123 2399*, Monday to Friday, 9am to 6pm

www.diabetes.org.uk/how_we_help/helpline


**Sickle Cell Society**

Support for those with the condition, including resources for young people

helpline@sicklecellsociety.org

Monday, Tuesday and Wednesday (10am-5pm) Valerie – 0780 973 6089

Thursday and Friday (10am-5pm) Sheri – 0208 963 7794


**Refuge**

www.refuge.org.uk/get-help-now/for-teenage-girls/

Freephone 24-Hour National Domestic Abuse Helpline: 0808 2000 247

www.nationaldahelpline.org.uk (access live chat Mon-Fri 3-10pm)


**Shelter**

Charity working for people in housing need by providing free, independent, expert housing advice

shelter.org.uk/youngpeople

## Young Stonewall

Information and support for all young lesbian, gay, bi and trans people.
0800 050 2020

youngstonewall.org.uk


## The Terence Higgins Trust

Growing up and entering the world of sex and relationships can seem confusing and worrying at first. If you are not sure if you are gay, lesbian, bisexual or transgender, you may find it helpful to talk to someone you trust about your feelings. – THT is there to answer your questions and give you some support.

Freephone:  0800 802 1221

www.tht.org.uk


## Grief Encounter

Supporting bereaved children and young people.
0808 802 0111 ,Weekdays 9am-9pm

grieftalk@griefencounter.org.uk

www.griefencounter.org.uk


## Children's Society

Help refugees and migrants.
www.childrenssociety.org.uk/what-we-do/our-work/young-refugees-migrants


## Red Cross

Different languages to help young refuges aged 15-25.

www.redcross.org.uk/get-help/get-help-as-a-young-refugee-or-asylum-seeker

Help if you are over 25 years old.

www.redcross.org.uk/get-help/get-help-as-a-refugee

### Young Roots

A website with help and activities based in Croydon and Brent Cross for Refugees.

www.youngroots.org.uk

### Refugee Support Network

www.refugeesupportnetwork.org/pages/2-our-services

### REAP

http://reap.org.uk/useful-websites-for-refugee-groups/

### UNHCR (The UN Refugee Agency)

www.unhcr.org/uk/useful-links.html

### Gingerbread

Helpline for single mothers and young fathers 0808 802 0925.

www.gingerbread.org.uk

### Working families

Information on what you are entitled to at university whilst pregnant.

www.workingfamilies.org.uk/articles/pregnancy-and-maternity-for-students/

www.ingramcontent.com/pod-product-compliance
Lightning Source LLC
Chambersburg PA
CBHW051805040426
42446CB00007B/533